DRIED RICE PAPER

These round edible wrappers are made from rice flour, salt, and water and come in varying sizes and shapes. They are tissue-thin and very brittle and have an imprint of a bamboo crisscross pattern on each sheet, left by the bamboo trays on which the papers are dried. They need to be softened with water before using; see Barbecued Beef Salad Wrapped in Rice Paper, page 69.

LOTUS LEAVES

Like banana leaves, these large (11-inch to 14-inch) leaves are used for both wrapping and flavoring food. They come dried and must be soaked overnight before using. For some dishes, cutting out the middle stem makes the folding and wrapping easier. Discard the stem.

SUI MAI SKINS

Sui mai skins are 3-inch round won ton skins that are rolled extra thin. A one-pound package contains 80 to 100 skins. Like other fresh pasta-style wrappers, they are ready to use straight from the package. Wrap the unused portion in an airtight plastic wrap or bag and store refrigerated for a few days or frozen for a few months. Thaw for 30 minutes before using.

WHEAT STARCH WRAPPERS

Wheat starch wrappers are unique because of their slightly gummy texture and translucence. They are made from wheat starch, a flour from which the gluten has been removed. These wrappers lack elasticity; make certain they are rolled thin, or the cooked skins will be rubbery.

WON TON SKINS

Won ton skins are made from a delicate pasta dough of egg, flour, and water. They are rolled into sheets ranging from

extra thin to thin to medium squares. A 1-pound package tains 80 to 100 skins, while t 60 to the pound. Store in the same way as *sui mai* wrappers, above. Freeze the unused portion.

Noodles

DRIED BEAN THREAD NOODLES

Dried bean thread noodles look like brittle, thin, white threads wound up into a bundle. They are often simmered with meats and vegetables, served cold in salads, or cooked in soups. They can also be simply boiled and immersed in soup or deep-fried in their dried state to make puffy, crisp noodles.

Bean thread noodles are marketed under several names, including transparent, cellophane, glass, mirror, peastarch, and mung bean noodles. They are made from pureed mung beans, strained and dried into sheets or noodles. I prefer to buy the 8-pack bags of individually wrapped 1.5-ounce bundles. There are many times when you need only a few ounces, and it is impossible to break down a large package without soaking the whole bundle in water first. Store the dry noodles in an airtight plastic bag in a dry cupboard. Do not confuse them with dried rice noodles, which look somewhat similar.

To prepare bean thread noodles, place the required amount of noodles in a bowl. Cover with warm water and soak for 20 to 30 minutes or until the noodles are soft and pliable. Drain. The noodles are ready to stir-fry, simmer, or add to soups. When cooked they become transparent and gelatinous. Bean thread noodles may be simmered for longer than other noodles without becoming mushy; they taste equally good reheated.

DRIED RICE NOODLES

Often referred to as rice stick noodles or rice vermicelli, these dried noodles are made from rice flour. There are two major shapes, one a skinny, round noodle, the other a flat noodle ¼ to ½ inch wide. Before being stir-fried or added to soups they must be softened in water until pliable. Deep-fried dry, the skinny noodles puff up into crisp, white noodles that are good for salads or as a bed for stir-fried meats and vegetables (see Crisp Rice Stick Noodles, page 26). Store dried noodles in a dry cupboard.

FRESH CHINESE EGG NOODLES

Chinese egg noodles are found in almost all American supermarkets. You are most likely to find the medium width. These are all-purpose noodles for stir-frying, deep-frying, soups, and cold noodle dishes. They are made from wheat flour, eggs, and water.

Thin egg noodles contain more egg than medium-width noodles. The extra egg gives a heartier texture, making them better for soups and chilled noodle dishes. In a pinch thin noodles can also be stir-fried or shallow-fried, but sauces tend to cling to the surface rather than being absorbed into the noodle.

Store fresh egg noodles in the refrigerator for up to a week or freeze them for up to 3 months. You do not need to thaw frozen noodles; simply take them out of the freezer and add them to boiling salted water. Stir continuously with chopsticks until the strands are separated.

To cook 1 pound of noodles, bring 4 quarts of salted water to a boil in a wok or large stockpot over high heat. Gently pull the ball of noodles apart to separate the strands. Add the noodles to the water and stir with long chopsticks until the water reaches a second boil. Add 1 cup of cold water to the pot. Continue cooking until the water returns to a boil. Pour the noodles into a colander and rinse with cold water. Drain thoroughly. Transfer to a large bowl and toss with sesame oil.

FRESH RICE NOODLES

Fresh rice noodles are immensely popular among Asians. They have a soft, silky smooth texture and look like thick white ribbons. They are made from rice powder that is made into a milk-like batter then steamed in flat stretched-cloth trays or shallow, round pizza-like trays. The noodle ribbons can be stir-fried or added to soup. Whole sheets of rice noodle can be wrapped around a shrimp or meat filling like cannelloni. Fresh rice noodles are available in Asian grocery stores and noodle shops. Keep them refrigerated and use them within 5 days. They cannot be frozen.

Oils

ASIAN HOT CHILI OIL

Hot chili oil is an infusion of hot chiles in vegetable oil. It is indispensable for adding a jolt to your food. Add just a few drops to season dumplings, sauces, and dressings. Commercially prepared brands vary in heat. It is easily made at home; just make certain you have good ventilation.

Heat 1 cup of peanut or corn oil until hot but not smoking. Reduce the heat to low and add a dozen whole dried red chiles, or more depending upon your taste. Stir for a minute, turn off the heat, and allow the oil to cool. Strain the oil into a container and discard the chiles. Refrigerated, the oil will keep for several weeks.

ASIAN SESAME OIL

Asian sesame oil is pressed from toasted white sesame seeds, which give it a strong nutty flavor and aroma. It is used sparingly as a seasoning oil and is not meant for cooking.

PEANUT OIL

Peanut oil is the preferred Asian cooking oil because of its high smoking point and neutral flavor. However, corn oil is also exceptionally good for Asian cooking.

Sauces, Pastes, and Condiments

ASIAN SESAME PASTE

This "nut butter" made from roasted sesame seeds is used as a base for dressings in cold salads. Refrigerated after opening it will keep indefinitely.

BASIC RED CURRY PASTE

There are many variations of Thai red curry paste. Here is a basic all-purpose one for the recipes in this book that you can make at home. Make more than you need; it freezes very well.

The first time you make the recipe you may have to try every electrical chopper, grinder, blender, spice mill, and mini-food processor in your kitchen. Use whatever works. Chop or grind each ingredient individually and remove it before chopping the next.

> *½ ounce dried red chiles*
> *6 strips dried kaffir lime rind*
> *4 quarter-size slices dried galangal*
> *2 stalks fresh lemongrass*
> *1 teaspoon whole coriander seeds*
> *½ teaspoon whole cumin seeds*
> *1 teaspoon whole black pepper*
> *½ teaspoon salt*
> *4 cloves garlic, chopped*
> *2 small shallots*
> *3 coriander roots, chopped*
> *1 teaspoon shrimp paste*
> *1 to 2 tablespoons water*

1. Crack the chiles and shake out the seeds. Place the chiles, lime rind, and galangal in separate small bowls. Cover each with warm water until soft and pliable, about 30 minutes. Drain. Cut off and discard the green tops from the lemongrass; remove and discard the tough outer leaves until you see a purple ring. Coarsely chop the tender stalk and set aside.

2. Toast the coriander seeds, cumin, pepper, and salt in an ungreased skillet over medium heat until fragrant, about 3 minutes. Pound or grind the seeds into a fine powder in a mortar or spice mill. Set aside.

3. Process the chopped lemongrass in a mini-food processor until as fine as possible. Remove to a bowl. Chop the softened galangal and lime rind as fine as possible and add them to the lemongrass. Chop the chiles as fine as possible. Leave the chiles in the processor. Add the garlic, shallots, coriander roots, shrimp paste, dry spice blend, and lemongrass mixture. Process into a paste. Pour water down the feed tube to facilitate the chopping. Transfer the paste to a mortar. Pound for 1 minute or until completely smooth. Makes about ⅓ cup.

BROWN BEAN SAUCE

This dark brown, thick cooking condiment is made from yellow soybean puree. It is used to impart a distinctive savory flavor. When the jar or can is labelled "Ground Brown Bean," it contains a puree; when labelled "Bean Sauce," it contains a paste with some whole beans. Brown bean sauce will keep indefinitely refrigerated in a sealed jar.

CHICKEN STOCK

As used in this book, "chicken stock" means a lightly seasoned broth made with just chicken, ginger, green onions, and a bit of salt. Many Asian cooks use Swanson canned chicken broth diluted with water to their taste. If using an unsalted stock, you may need to adjust the seasoning in a recipe with a little more salt, soy sauce, or fish sauce.

CHILI PASTE WITH GARLIC

This is similar to Hot Bean Sauce but contains more chiles and garlic. It is used sparingly as a cooking condiment. There are many varieties, each having its own flavor. Refrigerated it will keep indefinitely.

CHINESE HOT MUSTARD

Chinese hot mustard is made from Colman's dry mustard. Mix 2 tablespoons of the dry mustard with enough water to make a smooth, thick paste. Add a pinch each of sugar and salt and a dribble of peanut oil. Mix well and transfer to a dipping bowl. Cover. Let sit for 10 minutes.

COCONUT MILK
AND COCONUT CREAM

A principal ingredient in Thai cooking, coconut is used in desserts, curry preparations, soups, salads, vegetable entrees, and sauces. Coconut milk is not the water found in the middle of a coconut, but a rich liquid that is extracted by mixing the grated white flesh with hot water. Coconut milk is an essential ingredient in Southeast Asian cuisines; its presence is a distinguishing feature of Thai curries. A number of recipes in this book call for canned unsweetened coconut milk. The brands from Thailand are very good. Store leftover coconut milk in a plastic container or locking plastic bag; it can be refrigerated for a few days or frozen for several weeks.

For *coconut cream,* pour the contents of the can into a tall glass container. Let it sit until the liquid separates, then skim off the "cream" that has risen to the top. The liquid that has settled to the bottom may be used as thin coconut milk.

For *thick coconut milk,* shake the can before opening and use as is.

For *medium coconut milk,* dilute thick coconut milk with half as much water.

For *thin coconut milk,* dilute thick coconut milk with an equal amount of water.

FISH SAUCE,
THAI AND VIETNAMESE

Nam pla is the Thai name and *nuoc mam* is the Vietnamese name for fish sauce, the Southeast Asian equivalent of soy sauce. It is translucent, dark brown, and very thin with a salty flavor. Its pungent smell dissipates during cooking. Fish sauces vary from country to country; if possible, use the one from the country in which a particular dish originated. Store fish sauce in the cupboard in an airtight container; it will keep indefinitely.

GOLDEN MOUNTAIN SAUCE

Golden Mountain Sauce is a Thai brand of soy sauce used primarily for cooking rather than as a table sauce. Its flavor, not as salty or rich as other soy sauces, is distinctly suited for Thai cooking. Store like fish sauce and soy sauce.

HOISIN SAUCE

This popular table and cooking condiment is made from a reddish-brown type of soybean. It is quite sweet and is best known as the sauce served with Peking Duck and Mu Shu Pork. It is particularly good as part of a marinade for roasted and barbecued meats. It is often incorrectly referred to as Duck Sauce. If purchased in a jar, store in the refrigerator after opening; if it comes in a can, transfer it to a jar and refrigerate. It will keep indefinitely in the refrigerator.

HOT BEAN SAUCE

This popular Sichuan cooking condiment is a basic brown bean sauce infused with chile peppers. It will keep indefinitely if transferred from its opened can to a well-sealed jar in the refrigerator.

KETJAP MANIS

This thick, sweetened and spiced soy sauce is frequently used in Indonesian cooking. *Ketjap* means "a sauce added to food to enhance the flavor." It is the word from which the all-American "ketchup" is derived. In a tightly sealed bottle, it will keep indefinitely at room temperature.

MIRIN

This Japanese sweet cooking wine is used to add a mild sweetness to foods. Do not substitute saké for mirin.

OYSTER SAUCE

This dipping sauce and cooking condiment is made from oysters, water, and salt. It has a strong, pungent, salty flavor that is not at all fishy. Think of oyster sauce as a high-quality bouillon cube; a few teaspoons added to a dish seasons and enhances the sauce. Look for brands that are not pasty or lumpy-thick. Refrigerated, it will keep indefinitely.

PICKLED GARLIC

Pickled garlic is made from whole baby garlic heads marinated in a sweet, sour, and salt brine. Like pickles, it makes a great appetizer and is also used as a condiment or part of a relish. It is available in Southeast Asian markets.

JAPANESE-STYLE RICE VINEGAR

Asian vinegars tend to be milder in acidity and sweeter in flavor than Western vinegars. If rice vinegar is not available, substitute cider vinegar—dilute with a little water and add a bit of sugar to sweeten it.

SAKÉ

Saké is Japanese rice wine. It is used as a beverage and, in small quantities, for cooking.

SHAO HSING RICE WINE

This sherry-like Chinese wine is made from a mixture of glutinous rice, millet, and a special yeast. It is served as a warm beverage, but is also used in cooking. If unavailable, substitute a good dry sherry.

SHRIMP PASTE

Shrimp pastes (*kapi* in Thai) prepared from a fermented mixture of salt and shrimp are the basis of all good Southeast Asian cooking. Don't be put off by their pungent odor—it dissipates during cooking, leaving behind a subtle but distinctive flavor without which something will be missing from the dish.

There are two major types of shrimp paste, fresh and dried. The dried form is sold in compressed slabs or cakes, and is brown to almost black in color. To obtain the best flavor from the dried slabs, cut off the amount you need, wrap it in foil, and toast it in a dry skillet for two minutes before adding it to other ingredients.

The moister, "fresh" style of shrimp paste packed in jars requires no preparation. Since there is such a confusing variety of shrimp paste available, with many being poor quality, I suggest and prefer using a lavender-pink fresh shrimp paste packed in a jar from China or Hong Kong. I can depend on the quality, it is delicious and less pungent than the Southeast Asian varieties, and the package is convenient. This is the type I use for curry pastes, fried rice, and most other uses, although the very dark purple Thai fresh paste is delicious in the thicker style of Thai dipping sauces (*nam prik*). Fresh shrimp paste keeps indefinitely in the refrigerator. Anchovy paste makes a good substitute.

SICHUAN PRESERVED MUSTARD GREENS

This is a variety of mustard green native to Sichuan, pickled in salt and ground chiles. It comes canned and is often labelled Sichuan Preserved Vegetables. It has a salty and spicy taste, and a crunchy texture. It can be sliced, shredded, or minced for stir-fried, steamed, and braised dishes. Stored in a well-sealed container in the refrigerator, it will keep indefinitely. Rinse before using.

SOY SAUCE

Of the many varieties and grades of Chinese soy sauce, the two most commonly used are dark and light soy sauce. The dark is fermented longer, making it more flavorful and sweeter; light soy sauce tends to be more delicate and a little saltier. When cooking with soy sauce, think of it as you would red or white wine. Dark soy sauce, like red wine, goes better with meats and heartier foods. Light soy sauce is good with fish, shellfish, and poultry. Chinese cooks like to use a little of both in their cooking. Unless otherwise specified, "soy sauce" in the recipes means a Chinese-style dark soy sauce.

Japanese-style soy sauce contains more wheat; therefore it tends to be sweeter and less pungent, and should be used when cooking Japanese food. Soy sauce stores indefinitely in a dry cupboard.

SRIRACHA SAUCE

Sriracha sauce is a Southeast Asian-style prepared chili sauce made from pounded chiles, sugar, and vinegar. It is similar to Tabasco sauce, but slightly thicker, and it is used in the same fashion as a dipping condiment or for cooking.

TAMARIND

A fresh tamarind pod measures from 4 to 6 inches. It is solid, kiwi color, and looks like a pregnant green bean. The pulp is valued for its fruity sweet and sour flavor. The entire pod may be used in some dishes. Usually the pulp is soaked in hot water and pressed through a strainer to extract tamarind water, and the seeds and pulp discarded.

Preserved tamarind pulp, which still contains some of the seeds and fibers, is also available. Prepare it like the fresh pods. Another alternative is jars of tamarind concentrate which you dilute with hot water. Its flavor is satisfactory, but you should use it only in a pinch.

To make tamarind water, cover a 1-inch cube of tamarind pulp with ⅓ cup of boiling water. Mash the pulp and separate the fibers and seeds with the back of a fork. When dissolved, strain; reserve the liquid. Makes about ¼ cup.

THAI SPICY PEANUT CUCUMBER SAUCE

Serve this sauce with Spicy Fried Fish Cakes (page 33) or other deep-fried appetizers. The peanuts add an interesting crunchy texture.

> *½ cup white vinegar*
> *6 tablespoons sugar*
> *1 teaspoon salt*
> *½ cup water*
> *1 tablespoon Thai fish sauce* (nam pla)
> *1 serrano chile, chopped*
> *½ cucumber, peeled and thinly sliced*
> *1 teaspoon coarsely chopped fresh*
>   *coriander leaves*
> *3 tablespoons chopped roasted peanuts*

Simmer the vinegar, sugar, salt, and water until the sugar is dissolved. Cool. Add the fish sauce and chile. Put the cucumber slices in a small bowl, top with coriander leaves, and pour on the sweet vinegar sauce. Top with the peanuts. Makes about 1 cup.

THAI SWEET AND SOUR PLUM SAUCE

This sauce is wonderful with spring rolls and other fried appetizers. Chinese preserved plums can be found in Chinese, Southeast Asian, and Japanese grocery stores. Chinese children think of them as a candy. They are also used to season steamed spareribs and fish in Hong Kong and Thailand. They come dried or in a salt brine.

> *½ cup white vinegar*
> *⅓ cup sugar*
> *3 preserved plums in brine, pitted*

Bring the vinegar and sugar to a boil in a saucepan; boil to a thin syrup. Finely mince the plums and stir them in. Makes about ⅓ cup. Store in the refrigerator.

VIETNAMESE NUOC CHAM DIPPING SAUCE

This indispensable Vietnamese dipping sauce is used both at the table and in cooking.

> *4 cloves garlic*
> *2 fresh chiles, preferably serrano*
> *2 teaspoons sugar*
> *6 tablespoons Vietnamese fish sauce* (nuoc mam)
> *4 tablespoons fresh lime juice*
> *6 to 8 tablespoons water*

Grind the garlic, chiles, and sugar into a paste in a mortar, blender, or mini-food processor. Stir in the fish sauce and lime juice, and thin with water to taste. Strain into a dipping bowl.

Spices and Dried Ingredients

CHINESE SAUSAGES

These skinny, 6-inch-long sausages (*lop cheong*) are made from pork and a strong Chinese wine. They have a sweet flavor and a hard salami-like texture. There are two basic types, plain and one embedded with tiny bits of cured duck liver. They can be steamed and eaten as an appetizer, used as a main ingredient in casserole-style dishes, or stir-fried with vegetables. They are indispensable in Chinese and Southeast Asian cooking. They will keep for weeks in the refrigerator.

CHINESE DRIED BLACK MUSHROOMS

These mushrooms have come to be known by their Japanese name, *shiitake* mushrooms. A common Asian ingredient, they come in several varieties ranging from light tan to black in color. They are packaged in cellophane bags. The best grade are whole, perfectly shaped caps, light tan in color with a speckled flower-like pattern. They must be soaked in water, rinsed, drained, and squeezed dry before using. Cut off and discard the stems. The soaking water may be used in stocks or sauces. Store dried mushrooms in an airtight container.

CLOUD EARS

This small, black fungus comes in ½-inch dried pieces that are black and wrinkled. Cloud ears are sold under many names, including *wun yee*, tree ears, and black fungus. They come in two sizes, the smaller of which is more delicate and of a finer quality. Cloud ears have very little taste, but are prized for their crunchy texture and their ability to absorb flavors. When reconstituted in water, they triple in size; they may be cooked whole or torn apart.

DRIED OYSTERS

These oysters are preserved by drying them in the sun, which also concentrates their flavor. To reconstitute them, soak them in warm water overnight then rinse well to remove any sand and grit. They may be chopped or minced for stir-fried dishes, left whole for braised dishes, or used as a seasoning in soups. They are sold in bulk or in small packages. Tinned unflavored smoked oysters in oil are a good substitute.

DRIED CHILES

Several varieties of small dried chiles can be found in Asian and Latin American markets and in some supermarkets. Most common are the hot, skinny, 2-inch-long dried chiles simply labeled "hot red chile" or *chile japonés* in American markets. The Thai equivalent, called *prik haeng*, is slightly larger, about a finger's length, and less wrinkled.

To use dried chiles in curry pastes, crack them open and shake loose the seeds. Soak the chiles in warm water until softened, 20 to 30 minutes, before pounding them with other ingredients. Stored in an airtight container in a cool, dry place, they will keep indefinitely, although their color will fade.

DRIED SHRIMP

Drying concentrates the flavor of shrimp, making them a wonderful seasoning ingredient. Dried shrimp come in various sizes, the smallest called "rice-size shrimp." They can be found in the Asian and Mexican food sections of large supermarkets. Look for orange-pink dried shrimp about 1 inch long. Before using, soak them in warm water for 30 minutes, drain, and pat dry. Dried shrimp will keep indefinitely in a well-sealed container.

DRIED SHRIMP POWDER WITH CHILE

This is a seasoning powder made from pounded sun-dried shrimp with the addition of dried chile powder. Stored in an airtight container, it will keep indefinitely.

FIVE-SPICE POWDER

This pungent spice blend contains five or more spices, depending upon the manufacturer. Cinnamon, cloves, Sichuan peppercorns, star anise, and fennel are generally in the mixture. It is available in Asian markets. Use it for grilled or braised meats and poultry.

SICHUAN PEPPERCORNS

Sometimes referred to as *fagara*, these "peppercorns" are actually reddish-brown dried berries. They are not spicy, but they impart an unusual numbing sensation to the mouth. Look for packages of seeded peppercorns, since the husks are the desirable part. Before being used they need to be toasted, which triggers their distinctive flavor and aroma. Toast them in an ungreased wok over low heat until fragrant, about 5 minutes, stirring occasionally. Then crush the peppercorns in a mortar or use the bottom of a cleaver handle to pound them into a fine powder. Store in a well-sealed container for several weeks.

STAR ANISE

Star anise is a seed pod from a Chinese tree belonging to the magnolia family. Each star-shaped pod has eight points. Its pungent anise flavor is used to spice braised and simmered meat and poultry dishes.

TOASTED RICE POWDER

Ground toasted rice is used in Southeast Asia like bread crumbs in the West, as a thickener with a slight toasty flavor. Soak ½ cup of sweet glutinous rice in water for 1 hour. Drain well. Heat an ungreased skillet over medium heat. Add the rice and toast, stirring continuously, until golden brown, about 10 to 15 minutes. Cool. Transfer to a spice mill and grind to a fine powder (like sawdust). Strain through a fine-mesh sieve and discard the large grains. Store in an airtight jar in the refrigerator for up to 3 months.

Herbs and Aromatics

FRESH CHILES

Like dried chiles, small fresh chiles are essential to many Asian cuisines, and they come in many varieties. The most commonly available is the Mexican *chile serrano*: short, smooth-skinned, round-bodied and pointed on the end. The flesh has a very strong fresh flavor while the seeds and veins are loaded with heat. Serrano chiles have been adopted by the Thais (who call it *prik khee nu kaset*) and are used fresh for dips and cooking.

A Thai variety you might find here, known as *prik chee fah,* is about the size of a finger and comes in red, green, or yellow. They are hot but not overwhelming. They are quite similar to the fresh cayenne chile. This chile is sliced and used for cooking and also pounded into fresh dipping sauces.

The short, slender Thai "bird's eye" or "bird's beak" chiles are among the hottest chiles in the world. They are used as garnishes, to be nibbled on during a meal. They range in size from ½ to 2 inches long and sometimes have twisted bodies. Within this group of 3-alarm chiles, the *prik khee nu suan* is the smallest (barely 1 centimeter long, about the size of a rice grain) and the hottest.

Several recipes call for both red and green fresh chiles. All of the above varieties start out green and turn red when they ripen fully. I like to mix them not just for the sake of color, but for their subtle differences in flavor—the red versions are slightly sweeter and "fruitier" than the green.

Fresh chiles will keep for several weeks if kept dry, wrapped loosely in a brown paper bag or plastic bag and stored at the bottom of the refrigerator.

FRESH CORIANDER

Also known as Chinese parsley and cilantro, this herb is essential to Thai cooking. The leaves and stems are frequently used as an edible garnish. To clean fresh coriander, keep it in a bunch and submerge it in a basin of cold water, rinsing off the sand between the roots and stems. Still in a bunch, spin it in a lettuce drier.

Fresh Coriander Roots. In Thailand, fresh coriander comes with long, trailing, thin roots, often 4 to 5 inches long. They have a flavor reminiscent of fresh celery. They are difficult to find here, but are available in some markets. To use the roots, after washing the coriander cut the stems about 2 inches above where the stems and roots meet.

Freeze any roots you don't use so you'll have them for next time. Use just stems if roots are not available.

GALANGAL

Galangal is known as *kha* in Thailand, *laos* in Indonesia, and *lengkuas* in Malay, and sometimes as Indian ginger. This rhizome, a member of the ginger family, imparts a faint medicinal flavor and has a slight mustard fragrance. Dried slices and ground powder are available in Southeast Asian grocery stores. Always soak dried galangal in warm water until soft and pliable before using. It is virtually impossible to grind or chop it in a food processor before it is reconstituted in water. There is no substitute for galangal.

Fresh galangal is occasionally available in Asian markets. It looks a lot like ginger, but with stiff stalks rising vertically out of the rhizomes. If you can find it, use twice as much as the amount of dried galangal called for in the recipe. Scrape off the thin skin with a vegetable peeler. Store like fresh ginger, below. It will keep for a few weeks.

GINGER

Unless otherwise specified, "ginger" in this book means fresh ginger, which is sometimes referred to as green ginger. When a slice is called for in a recipe, cut a piece the size and thickness of an American quarter. I usually bruise or crush the slice by slapping it with the side of a cleaver, which helps release its flavor, juices, and aroma. Peel ginger before mincing, shredding, or grating. Ginger juice may be obtained by pressing ginger slices through a garlic press and catching the juice in a small bowl. Store ginger in a brown paper bag in the vegetable bin in the refrigerator. It will keep for several weeks.

KAFFIR LIME

This citrus is indigenous to Southeast Asia. Both the leaves and the lumpy green rind impart a perfume-like aroma, flavor, and oil to Thai food. The juice is not used. Before using dried kaffir rind, soak it in warm water until pliable. Kaffir lime leaves are used for flavoring in the same way as bay and curry leaves. They have a distinctive citrus fragrance and zesty taste, delicious in soups and sauces. Excellent frozen leaves from Thailand are available in better Southeast Asian markets. The leaves of a fresh American lime are an adequate substitute, but do try to locate the kaffir lime rind.

LEMON OR LIME ZEST

There are many gadgets available to peel the zest (the colored outer part of the skin) from a lemon or lime. My favorite method is to use a vegetable peeler, drawing it across the skin with very light pressure so that just the zest is removed, leaving the bitter white pith behind. The wide strips of zest can then be gathered up, stacked, and chopped.

LEMONGRASS

When I think of Thai food, lemongrass immediately comes to mind; it is an essential component in Thai cooking. Lemongrass is now available almost all year round in Asian markets. To use it, remove the tough fibrous outer leaves to get to the tender bulb-like heart. Dried stems of lemongrass are also available; they must be soaked in hot water before being used.

SHALLOTS

Shallots are considered the everyday onion in Southeast Asia. In foreign cookbooks they are often referred to as red or Bombay onions. An Asian shallot is half the size of an American shallot or smaller. Figure one American shallot for every 2 or 3 shallots called for in a foreign cookbook. The recipes in this book assume that you are using American shallots.

THAI BASIL

The variety of sweet basil used in Thai cooking (*bai horapha* or *bai horabha*) has small, flat, pointed green leaves with slightly serrated edges. The stems are sometimes reddish purple. Thai basil imparts a strong anise or licorice taste and, thus, is often referred to as "licorice basil." In Thai cooking basil is thought of as a leaf vegetable; it is particularly good in curry preparations and stir-fried entrees. If you can't find it, substitute another variety of sweet basil.

Accompaniments and Garnishes

The following is a collection of relishes, crunchy toppings, and other garnishes to add an extra element of flavor or texture to Asian-style dishes. Some are called for in specific recipes in this book, others are not; but all of them are handy to have in your cooking repertoire.

CHINESE SWEET PICKLED MUSTARD CABBAGE

Chilled Chinese pickled vegetables are often served as part of a dim sum lunch. They are similar to pickles but are made with mustard cabbage instead of cucumbers. They make a great side dish, a refreshing, crunchy appetizer, or a summer picnic treat. Make a big batch; it will keep for several weeks in the refrigerator. Look for mustard cabbage, a bulbous head with thick stems and broad, short leaves, in Asian markets.

> *¾ cup sugar*
> *½ cup white vinegar*
> *2 tablespoons salt*
> *1-inch lump ginger, peeled and bruised*
> *2 cloves garlic, bruised*
> *2 dried red chiles*

3 cups water
1½ pounds Chinese mustard cabbage
1 red bell pepper, seeded

Combine the sugar, vinegar, salt, ginger, garlic, chiles, and water in a saucepan; bring to a boil and cook until the sugar and salt dissolve. Cut the mustard cabbage stems and red bell pepper into ½-inch-wide chunks. Tear the cabbage leaves into 1-inch pieces. Put the vegetables in a large glass jar and pour the hot liquid over them. Allow the liquid to cool, then cover the jar and refrigerate for at least 1 day. Serve chilled. Makes about 1 quart.

CRISP FRIED SHALLOT AND GARLIC FLAKES

Cut 8 shallots or garlic cloves crosswise into ⅛-inch-thick slices; you should have ¾ cup of slices. The slices must all be of equal thickness to assure even cooking. Heat 2 cups of vegetable oil to 300° in a preheated wok, saucepan, or skillet. Add the slices and fry slowly for 3 to 5 minutes or until golden brown and crisp. They should be completely dry with no remaining moisture. Remove with a fine strainer and drain on paper towels. When cool, store in an airtight container. The flakes will keep for several weeks. Makes about ½ cup. The flavored oil can be strained and used for stir-frying.

CRISP LOTUS ROOT CHIPS

Deep-fried slices of fresh lotus root make an exotic garnish and a delicious snack food. Their intricate, lacy pattern makes an interesting conversation piece at a cocktail party. Lotus roots should be fried shortly after they are peeled or they will turn color. To prevent discoloration, put the slices into a bowl of water with vinegar or lemon juice (about 2 teaspoons vinegar per 1 quart water). Blot dry thoroughly before frying.

Peel fresh lotus roots with a vegetable peeler. Rinse with cold water and blot dry. Cut crosswise into ⅛-inch-thick slices. Heat 2 cups of vegetable oil to 375° in a pre-heated wok, saucepan, or skillet. Add the slices and fry until golden brown and crisp, about 1 minute. Drain on paper towels. Serve at room temperature.

CRISP RICE STICK NOODLES

The trick to successful deep-fried rice stick noodles is to fry small amounts with adequate hot oil. Rice stick noodles come in 1-pound packages containing four wafers. One wafer is sufficient for making a garnish.

1 wafer rice stick noodles
2 cups peanut oil

Inside a large paper bag pull the noodle wafer into 4 pieces. The bag will keep flying pieces of noodle from messing up your kitchen. Preheat a wok over medium-high heat. When hot, add the oil and heat it to 375°. Drop in one noodle strand to test the heat; it should puff up within 5 seconds. If it does not, the oil is not hot enough. (Continue heating and test again.) Add one portion of noodles to the oil. As soon as they puff, turn them over with chopsticks or tongs and fry the other side for 3 seconds. Immediately scoop them out and drain on paper towels. Repeat with the remaining noodles. You may fry noodles a few days in advance. Store in an airtight container.

OMELET SHREDS

Beat 2 eggs with a pinch of salt and pepper. Heat a non-stick skillet over medium-high heat. Add a bit of vegetable oil, wipe it over the pan with a paper towel, and wipe off the excess. Pour about ⅓ of the eggs into the middle of the pan. Tilt it in all directions to spread the egg evenly over the pan. When the egg is lightly browned, turn it over to brown the other side. Remove it to a cutting board. Repeat with the remaining egg. When cooled, roll the omelets up jelly-roll style and cut them crosswise into very thin slivers. Shake them loose. Use as a garnish.

PAPPADAMS

Pappadams are parchment-thin dried Indian wafers made from dal, any of the various dried beans, peas, or lentils used in Indian cooking. They come plain or laced with spices such as cracked black pepper. When cooked they inflate into crispy chip-like crackers. They can be served as a side dish, treated somewhat like bread with a full meal, or eaten as a snack between meals. (I enjoy them as a finger-food appetizer and find them very addicting.)

To prepare pappadam ribbon chips, cut the wafers with kitchen shears into 1-inch-wide strips or other shapes. (They tend to crack.) Heat 2 cups of vegetable oil in a pre-heated wok or saucepan to 375°. Add a few strips and push them under the oil with tongs. Deep-fry until they swell and are a very light golden brown, about 10 seconds. Drain on paper towels. They will seem limp, but will crisp up in a few seconds. Serve at room temperature.

SHRIMP CHIPS

Shrimp chips are the potato chips of Asia. Uncooked, they look like thick, dehydrated potato chips in a variety of colors. When they are deep-fried they expand to four times their size. Indonesian shrimp chips, *krupuk*, expand to the size of a plate. Shrimp chips are eaten like chips or used as an edible garnish or scoop.

To fry shrimp chips, heat 2 inches of vegetable oil in a wok or saucepan to 350°. Drop in a few chips. Use extra-long cooking chopsticks or tongs to keep the chips immersed in the oil. Fry for 5 to 10 seconds; the chips will puff up. Turn them over to make sure both sides are puffed. Drain on a tray lined with paper towels. If the chips do not expand within a few seconds, the oil is not hot enough. Start over. Serve chips at room temperature. Store leftovers in an airtight container; they will keep for 3 to 4 days.

THAI SWEET AND SOUR CUCUMBER RELISH

Use this sauce as a dipping sauce or a relish to accompany deep-fried foods.

> ½ teaspoon dried shrimp powder with chile (optional)
> ½ cup white vinegar
> ⅓ cup sugar
> 1 teaspoon salt
> ½ cup water
> 1 tablespoon Thai fish sauce (nam pla)
> 3 fresh red chiles, finely chopped
> ½ English hothouse cucumber
> 2 shallots
> 1 tablespoon coarsely chopped fresh coriander leaves, plus more for garnish

1. Toast the shrimp powder in an ungreased skillet until fragrant; set aside. Simmer the vinegar, sugar, salt, and water until the sugar dissolves. Cool. Add the fish sauce and chiles.

2. Peel the cucumber and cut it lengthwise into quarters. Cut each quarter crosswise into thin slices; arrange the slices in a shallow bowl. Peel the shallots and cut them into thin slices. Toss them with the cucumbers, dried shrimp powder, and coriander leaves.

3. Pour the liquid mixture over the cucumber and onions. Cover and refrigerate. Serve chilled or at room temperature as a dipping sauce, garnished with coriander. Makes about 2 cups.

TOASTED SESAME SEEDS

Set an ungreased skillet over medium heat. Add the desired amount of sesame seeds and toast until golden brown, about 3 minutes. Remove the seeds from the pan; set aside to cool.

HOT APPETIZERS

Pork Rib Tea Soup
Pan-Broiled Black Mushrooms
Spicy Fried Fish Cakes
Lemon Chicken Medallions
Curried Fish Mousse in a
	Banana Leaf Basket
Cheese and Sausage Panko Sticks
Minced Squab in Lettuce Cups
Cantonese Steamed Cracked Crab
Gold Coin Tea Sandwiches
Baked Barbecued Pork Buns
Shrimp-Stuffed Eggplant Sandwiches
Sesame Chicken Cakes
Hearts of Palm Spring Rolls
	(Lumpia Ubod)
Tonkatsu Fingers

Spicy Fried Fish Cakes
(recipe, pg. 33)

BAK KU TEH
Pork Rib Tea Soup
(Singapore)

Although most Asian lunches and dinners include a soup, there are certain soups which are served as a snack or even for breakfast. In Singapore, one of my favorite ways to start a day is to trek over to a hawker's stall and have a bowl of pork rib "tea" (actually a clear soup tinted with soy sauce). It comes with Chinese crullers for dunking, and a strong black tea which I think of as the "espresso" of teas. This recipe comes from the Straits Cafe in San Francisco. The crullers, baguette-shaped fried savory pastries, may be purchased at better Asian markets.

Serves 4 to 6

> *1 pound pork back ribs, chopped into*
>   *2-inch lengths*
> *1 large clove garlic, crushed*
> *6 cups water*
> *1 stick cinnamon*
> *3 whole star anise*
> *1 teaspoon whole white peppercorns*
> *1½ teaspoons sugar*
> *3 teaspoons salt*
> *3 tablespoons dark soy sauce, or to taste*

GARNISHES
2 tablespoons Crisp Fried Shallot Flakes (page 26)
Soy sauce and thinly sliced red chiles, for dipping
2 Chinese crullers, sliced (optional)
Steamed white rice

1.   Combine the pork, garlic, and water in a large saucepan; bring to a boil and cook for 5 minutes. Skim and discard the scum from the surface. Add the cinnamon, star anise, peppercorns, sugar, salt, and soy sauce. Reduce the heat to low and simmer until the pork is tender, about 45 minutes. Discard the excess fat from the soup before serving.

2.   Serve the soup in deep bowls with 3 to 4 rib pieces per serving and shallot flakes scattered over the top. Combine soy sauce and chiles to taste in small bowls as a dipping sauce for the ribs. Serve with cruller slices for dunking into the broth, and a bowl of rice on the side.

PAN-BROILED BLACK MUSHROOMS
(*China*)

These delicious mushrooms, braised in soy sauce and then seared in a hot skillet, are wonderful finger-food appetizers. The winy-sweet-savory flavors of the braising liquid accentuate the earthy flavor of the mushrooms, and a quick turn in the hot, dry skillet gives all the flavors an extra intensity. You can also slice them and stir-fry them with noodles, or serve them over rice as an accompaniment to tempura.

12 large (2-inch diameter) Chinese dried black
mushrooms
¾ cup chicken stock
2 tablespoons dark soy sauce
1 tablespoon sugar
2 tablespoons mirin
1 tablespoon vegetable oil (approximately)

1.   Soak the mushrooms in hot water until soft and pliable, about 20 minutes. Remove the mushrooms from the soaking liquid. Strain ½ cup of the liquid into a saucepan; add the chicken stock, soy sauce, sugar, and mirin and bring to a boil over medium-high heat. Add the mushrooms and simmer until the liquid is almost completely reduced, about 20 minutes. Allow the mushrooms to cool, then trim off and discard the stems. Flatten the mushrooms with a rolling pin to squeeze out the excess liquid.

2.   Preheat a cast-iron skillet over medium-high heat. Wad up several layers of paper towel and dip it into the oil; wipe a thin film of oil on the skillet. Lay the mushrooms in the skillet in a single layer. Pressing down on the mushrooms with a spatula, cook for 1 minute. Turn and cook 1 minute on the other side, again pressing with the spatula so the mushrooms come out dry. Serve hot with skewers or toothpicks.

VARIATION The mushrooms may be grilled over a hot charcoal fire, starting with the stem side down, about 1½ minutes per side. Use the same pressing technique.

TOD MUN
Spicy Fried Fish Cakes
(Thailand)

Unlike soft and feather-light Western quenelles, these Thai-style fish cakes are rather spongy and firm. Thinly sliced green beans incorporated into the fresh fish paste and a crisp surface from deep-frying add additional textures, and the kaffir lime leaf and red curry paste contribute appetite-arousing citrus and spice flavors.

Makes 12

> *½ pound ground fresh fish paste (see Note)*
> *1 teaspoon Basic Red Curry Paste (see page 18),*
> *   or commercially prepared curry paste*
> *¼ pound green beans, cut into ⅛-inch pieces*
> *1 clove garlic, pressed through a garlic press*
> *1 fresh kaffir lime leaf, stem and central*
> *   spine removed, finely shredded (optional)*
> *2 teaspoons cornstarch*
> *½ teaspoon salt*
> *Large pinch white pepper*
> *Vegetable oil for deep-frying*

1.   Combine all the ingredients except the vegetable oil. Wet your hands with cold water to keep the fish from sticking, then form the fish mixture into twelve 2-inch round patties, about ½ inch thick.

2.   Preheat a wok or deep saucepan; when hot, add vegetable oil to a depth of 2 inches; heat the oil to 360°. Dip a long pastry knife or metal spatula into the oil, slip it under a fish cake, and carefully lower the cake into the oil. Add as many cakes as will fit and float freely and fry, turning once, until the cakes are well browned on both sides and float to the surface, 3 to 4 minutes. Remove the cakes and drain on paper towels. Serve hot with Thai Spicy Peanut Cucumber Sauce (see page 21).

NOTE Ready-made ground fresh fish paste is available in better Asian fish markets. Look for one that is not pre-seasoned; if it is already seasoned (the best way to tell is to cook a bit and taste it), reduce the salt or other seasonings in the recipe accordingly. You can make your own paste by grinding ½ pound of any white-fleshed fish fillets to a puree in a food processor, then adding 1 beaten egg white and incorporating it with a pulsing action.

LEMON CHICKEN MEDALLIONS
(China)

These light, crisp, tender pan-fried chicken medallions are served with a subtle yet zesty sweet-and-sour sauce, enhanced by a bit of gin.

Serves 6 to 8 as a first course

3 large chicken breast halves, boned (about 1 pound)
3 tablespoons gin
1 tablespoon light soy sauce
½ teaspoon salt
¼ teaspoon sugar
Peanut or corn oil for pan-frying
Lemon slices, for garnish

ZESTY LEMON-GIN SAUCE
4 tablespoons fresh lemon juice
2 tablespoons gin
1 teaspoon grated ginger
1½ tablespoons sugar
1 tablespoon honey
½ teaspoon salt
Zest of one lemon, cut into thin slivers
1½ teaspoons water chestnut flour (see Note) or cornstarch
¼ cup chicken stock

BATTER
3 large egg whites
3 tablespoons water chestnut flour or all-purpose flour
3 tablespoons cornstarch
1 tablespoon black sesame seeds
1 teaspoon salt

1.   Skin the chicken breasts and cut them across the grain into ½-inch-thick slices. Pound each slice with the side of a cleaver to flatten it into an oval medallion about ¼ inch thick. Combine the gin, soy sauce, salt, and sugar in a bowl; add the chicken and marinate for 20 minutes.

2.   Prepare the Zesty Lemon-Gin Sauce as follows: Combine the lemon juice, gin, ginger, sugar, honey, salt, and lemon zest in a saucepan. Cook over high heat until the sugar and honey are dissolved. Stir the water chestnut flour and chicken stock together to make a smooth paste; stir the paste into the sauce and cook until thickened. Keep warm.

3.   Heat the oven to 200°. To make the batter, beat the egg whites until frothy. Combine the water chestnut flour, cornstarch, sesame seeds, and salt and blend them lightly into the egg whites; do not overstir. Preheat a skillet over medium-high heat and add enough oil to coat the bottom. Drain the chicken medallions, and add the drained marinade to the sauce. Coat the chicken pieces with batter. Place a few medallions in the skillet, not touching each other. Fry until the bottoms are crisp and golden brown; turn them over and brown the other side (about 3 minutes total). The chicken should feel firm to the touch. Transfer to a serving plate and keep warm in the oven while you cook the remaining medallions.

4.   Reheat the sauce and pour it over the chicken. Garnish with the lemon slices. Serve hot.

NOTE Many Chinese cooks prefer to use water chestnut flour in place of cornstarch or flour as a coating or as part of a batter for deep-frying. It produces a lighter and crisper texture. It also serves exceptionally well as a thickening agent in place of cornstarch. The flour is made from ground water chestnuts and is sold in plastic bags. It will keep indefinitely in an airtight container.

HAW MOK
Curried Fish Mousse
in a Banana Leaf Basket
(Thailand)

In Asian cooking, pâté-like dishes are steamed, not baked in a bain-marie as they are in the West. The resulting texture is the same—dense and moist—but this fish loaf with its array of aromatic Thai spices would never be mistaken for a French mousse. Chicken is a delicious alternative to the fish.

With its curry flavoring and thick coconut topping, the mousse doesn't really need a sauce; but if you want an even more extravagant presentation, heat the remaining coconut milk from the second can with a couple of teaspoons of red curry paste and simmer until thick and creamy, then season to taste with fish sauce and palm sugar.

Serves 8

> 2¾ cups unsweetened coconut milk
> ½ tablespoon rice flour
> ½ tablespoon Basic Red Curry Paste (page 18)
>   or commercially prepared red curry paste
> 1 pound fresh ground fish paste (see Note,
>   page 33)
> 1 egg, beaten
> 2 tablespoons Thai fish sauce (nam pla)
> 1 green onion (including top), chopped
> 1 tablespoon chopped coriander leaves
> ½ cup chopped Thai sweet basil (horapha),
>   plus 1½ cups whole leaves
> 3 tablespoons finely shredded fresh or frozen kaffir
>   lime leaf (if not available, substitute fresh
>   citrus leaves)
> 1 package frozen banana leaves, or 2 fresh leaves
> 2 red serrano chiles, seeded and finely sliced

1.   Open one of the cans of coconut milk without shaking it. Pour the contents into a tall glass container and allow it to separate. Skim ¾ cup of the coconut cream off the top and put it into a saucepan with the rice flour. Bring to a boil, stirring, and remove from the heat. Set aside. This is the topping.

2.   Combine ½ cup of the remaining coconut milk with the curry paste in a small saucepan and simmer for 5 minutes. Remove from the heat and set aside to cool.

3.   To prepare the mousse, combine the ground fish paste, egg, fish sauce, green onion, half the coriander leaves, the chopped basil leaves, half the shredded lime leaves, and the curry paste mixture in a bowl; mix well. Gradually stir 1½ cups coconut milk into the mixture. You should have about 4 cups mixture.

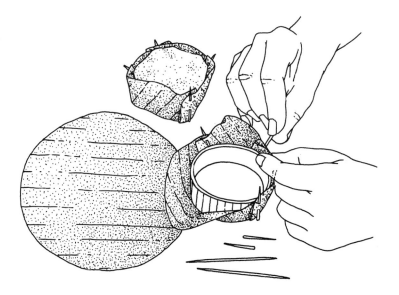

Forming a banana leaf basket

4.   Rinse the banana leaves with cold water and wipe thoroughly. Cut out sixteen 5½-inch-diameter rounds. Dip the rounds in boiling water for a few seconds to soften them; drain and pat dry. For each basket, lay 2 rounds together with the dull sides facing each other. Set a 2½-inch-wide custard cup in the middle of the circle (to serve as a mold), and pull both leaves up and around it. Make 4 equally spaced pleats around the edge, to shape the rounds into a bowl. Secure the pleats with toothpicks or staples and remove the custard cup; the leaves should form a free-standing basket. Repeat with the remaining leaves.

5.   Divide the remaining basil leaves among the banana-leaf baskets; fill the baskets with the fish paste mixture. Set the baskets in a bamboo steaming basket (you may need to use two tiers) or on a steaming rack. Set in a wok over boiling water, cover, and steam for 15 minutes, or until the mousse is firm to the touch and a toothpick inserted in the center comes out clean. Remove the banana baskets from the steamer. Spoon a little of the coconut topping into each basket and top with the remaining lime leaves, sliced chile, and coriander leaves. Serve hot or cold.

CHEESE AND SAUSAGE PANKO STICKS
(East/West)

Although cheese is not part of the traditional Asian diet, I enjoy combining mild cheeses such as Monterey Jack and mozzarella with Asian ingredients and cooking techniques. Here the mild flavor and creamy consistency of Monterey Jack cheese complements the delicate sweet, winy flavor of Chinese sausages. Simple to prepare, the finished sticks taste like cheese fondue croquettes. If you prefer a bit more gusto, dip the cheese sticks in tonkatsu sauce, a com-

mercially prepared Japanese sauce a little like a mixture of Worcestershire and catsup. Panko, Chinese sausage, and tonkatsu sauce are all available in Asian grocery stores.

Makes 12

> 2 *Chinese sausages* (lop cheong)
> 10- to 12-ounce block Monterey Jack cheese
> 2 large eggs, lightly beaten
> 1 teaspoon water
> **Pinch of salt**
> ½ cup all-purpose flour
> 1 cup fine panko (Japanese bread crumbs) or
>   bread crumbs
> Vegetable oil for deep-frying
> Tonkatsu sauce (optional)

1.   Prepare a wok for steaming (see page 13). Place the sausages on a heatproof plate and set it on a steaming tray or rack. Steam over medium-high heat for 10 minutes. Remove from the wok and cool. Cut the sausages diagonally into very thin slices. Set aside.

2.   Cut the cheese into twelve sticks 1 inch wide by 3 inches long by ½ inch thick. Lay the sticks flat and cut a 2-inch-long slit through the middle of each, leaving the ends uncut. Stuff 2 or 3 slices of sausage into each slit.

3.   Beat the eggs with water and salt. Dip each cheese stick in flour, then roll it the egg mixture, thoroughly coating it and leaving no dry areas. Roll the stick in panko and gently pat the crumbs in place. Set the coated sticks on a cookie sheet lined with waxed paper; refrigerate, loosely covered, for 2 hours or more.

4.   Pour 2 inches of oil into a wok or deep frying pan; heat to 375°. Place the cheese sticks a few at a time into the hot oil; deep-fry until crisp and golden brown, about 1 minute. Remove with a slotted spoon and drain on paper towels. Serve hot as a finger food appetizer or as a first course.

MINCED SQUAB
IN LETTUCE CUPS
(China)

Squab, often a euphemism for pigeon, was not always the esteemed bird it is today. I suspect that in the past pigeon, though not particularly tender, was abundant and therefore more affordable than chicken or other birds. Mincing the meat preserved its flavor while minimizing its toughness. Today's farmed squab has a much finer texture, but it maintains some of the gamey flavor that goes so well with the other ingredients in this dish.

Although this recipe may seem laborious, once the preparation is done, the actual cooking takes less than 8 minutes, and the results are well worth the modest effort.

Serves 6

> 4 small dried oysters, or tinned smoked
>   oysters in oil
> 1 head iceberg or butter lettuce
> ½ cup Hoisin Dipping Sauce (see Note)
> 2 cups Crisp Rice Stick Noodles (page 26)
> 6 dried Chinese black mushrooms
> 2 large squabs (about 12 ounces each)

SQUAB MARINADE
> 2 teaspoons Shao Hsing wine or dry sherry
> 2 teaspoons soy sauce
> ¼ teaspoon sugar
> 1 teaspoon cornstarch
> 1 teaspoon Asian sesame oil

> ✿

> 1 teaspoon cornstarch
> 2 teaspoons oyster sauce
> 2 tablespoons peanut or corn oil
> ½ teaspoon salt
> 2 teaspoons finely minced or grated ginger

> 3 green onions (including tops), finely chopped
> ½ pound fresh water chestnuts, peeled and
>   minced
> ½ cup finely minced bamboo shoots
> ¼ teaspoon sugar
> **Large pinch white pepper**
> 2 teaspoons soy sauce
> 1 teaspoon Asian sesame oil

1. If using dried oysters, soak them at least 2 hours ahead of time or overnight. When soft, rinse and pat dry.

2. While the oysters are soaking, prepare the accompaniments. If using iceberg lettuce, core the head and discard the heart. Submerge the lettuce in cold water to loosen the leaves. One by one, carefully remove 12 whole leaves. Trim each leaf with scissors into a 3-inch cup. If using butter lettuce, wash and separate the leaves and choose 12 that are cup shaped. Wrap the lettuce leaves in a towel and refrigerate until chilled. Prepare the dipping sauce and crisp noodles as directed.

3. Cover the mushrooms with water and soak until soft and pliable, about 20 minutes. Meanwhile, skin and bone the squabs. Mince the meat finely and evenly. Combine the marinade ingredients in a bowl; toss with the squab, and set aside.

4. Remove the mushrooms from the soaking liquid (reserve the liquid) and squeeze out the excess. Cut off and discard the stems and finely mince the caps. Combine the cornstarch and oyster sauce with 2 tablespoons of the reserved mushroom soaking liquid; mix to a smooth paste. Set aside. Drain and mince the oysters.

5. Have all the minced, marinated, and liquid ingredients ready near the stove. Preheat a wok over medium-high heat. When hot, add 2 teaspoons of the oil or just enough to coat the sides of the wok. Wipe off the excess. Add the squab. Toss and stir the meat, breaking up the lumps, until all the

excess liquid is cooked away and the meat is dry and crumbly. Push the meat up the sides of the wok. Pour the remaining oil in the center. Add the salt, ginger, and half of the green onions. Toss and stir them with the squab.

6.   Increase the heat to high. One at a time add the oysters, black mushrooms, water chestnuts, and bamboo shoots; stir-fry each as it is added for about 30 seconds. Add the sugar, pepper, and soy sauce; toss together for 10 seconds. Add the reserved cornstarch mixture; stir and toss until the mixture holds together. Dribble in the sesame oil. Transfer the squab mixture to the middle of a good-sized platter. Scatter the remaining green onions on top. Crush the noodles and add to the platter in a ring around the squab mixture. Arrange the lettuce cups around the edge.

7.   To eat, put 2 tablespoons of noodles in the center of a lettuce cup. Put 2 tablespoons of the squab mixture over the noodles. Top with 1 teaspoon of the dipping sauce, roll the cup in your hand, and take a bite.

NOTE To make Hoisin Dipping Sauce, dilute Hoisin Sauce with enough hot water to give it a creamy consistency. Season to taste with sugar and a few drops of sesame oil.

TECHNIQUE NOTE All the filling ingredients must be very finely chopped. Too coarse a texture detracts from the delicacy of the dish.

CANTONESE STEAMED CRACKED CRAB
(*China*)

To the Cantonese there is only one acceptable kind of crab, and that is one that is alive and kicking right up to the moment of cooking. When crab is that fresh, steaming is my favorite cooking method, and a simple dipping sauce made with white wine vinegar is the perfect accompaniment. On the West Coast where I live, Dungeness crab is a favorite of the local Chinese (the months of the year that contain the letter R are crab season). For a quick light meal for two, serve cracked crab with stir-fried spinach, kale, or other vegetables.

Serves 4

> *1 live crab, about 2½ pounds*
> *2 whole green onions*
> *2 quarter-size slices ginger*
> *1 tablespoon Shao Hsing wine or dry sherry*

GINGER SCALLION DIPPING SAUCE
2 tablespoons finely shredded ginger
¼ teaspoon sugar
½ teaspoon salt
¼ cup finely shredded green onion (including tops)
5 tablespoons white wine vinegar
3½ tablespoons peanut oil

1.   Prepare a wok for steaming (see page 13). Rinse and kill the crab and place it shell side down on a heat-resistant plate. Put the remaining ingredients on top of the crab and place the plate on the steaming rack over the boiling water. Steam over high heat for 15 minutes. Remove and cool.

2. While the crab cools, make the dipping sauce. Scatter the ginger in a shallow saucer. Sprinkle the sugar and salt evenly over it. Scatter the green onions on top and pour on the vinegar. Heat the oil to hot but not smoking, then pour it on top. It should make a sizzling sound.

3. Disjoint and crack the crab (see below) and arrange the pieces on a platter. To eat, use the tip of a leg to pick out the meat. Dip the meat into the dipping sauce.

TECHNIQUE NOTE To clean a crab, first put it in the sink and rinse it in cold water. With a long-handled brush, scrub the underside and between the claws and legs (watch out for the claws!) to remove any sand and grit. Rinse again. For humanitarian reasons, I prefer to kill the crab quickly by plunging it into boiling water before preparing it further. Another method is to hold the crab firmly against a work surface and stab it just behind the eyes with a knife, which kills it instantly. The crab is now ready for cooking.

   To disjoint and crack a cooked crab (or to prepare an uncooked crab for stir-frying), first lift the triangular apron on the underside with the tip of a knife (figure 1); grasp the apron and remove it with a twisting motion, drawing out the intestinal tube with it. Hold the top shell in one hand, gather the legs and claws on one side of the crab in the other hand, and gently tug until the top shell comes free from the body and legs (figure 2). Discard the feathery gills on each side of the body and the mandibles at the "face" end. Now gently bend back the legs and claws and twist them free. You are left with the body section, with the creamy yellow tomalley (greenish in an uncooked crab) in the center. Spoon it out and reserve it for those who appreciate it. Chop the body down the center with a cleaver, then cut each half crosswise into three equal pieces (figure 3). Crack each leg and claw section with a light hammer or nutcracker (figure 4).

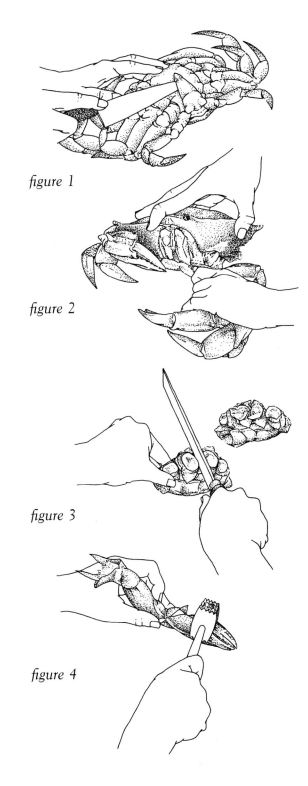

figure 1

figure 2

figure 3

figure 4

GOLD COIN
TEA SANDWICHES
(China)

I grew up never questioning why these tea sandwiches were called Gold Coin Buns. They were stuffed with thin slices of honey-glazed barbecued pork or honey-glazed barbecued fresh bacon, neither of which resembled coins. When I ordered the dish in Hong Kong, I got a skewer of alternating slices of golden brown, coin-shaped, glazed barbecued pork, liver, and fresh bacon, but no buns. They were two totally different dishes; both are marvelous. This recipe is the one I grew up with. The sandwiches look great on a buffet table.

Plan to marinate the meat for 8 hours or overnight. Both the pork slices and the buns can be made in advance and refrigerated or frozen.

Makes 24

> 1½ to 2 pounds boneless pork loin or
>   pork butt (see Note)
> 2 tablespoons Shao Hsing wine or dry sherry
> 2 tablespoons hoisin sauce
> ¼ cup dark soy sauce
> 3 tablespoons sugar
> 1 teaspoon grated ginger
> ½ cup honey
> 24 Steamed Gold Coin Sandwich Buns (page 43)
> 1½ tablespoons water
> 1 or 2 green onions (white and pale green
>   parts), cut into 2-inch slivers

1.   You may want to freeze the pork for 1 hour to make thin slicing easier; it should feel firm but not frozen. Trim off any excess fat (before freezing if you freeze it). Cut the pork across the grain into ⅛-inch-thick slices, approximately 2 inches by 3½ inches. If you use pork butt, you may need

to cut it in half lengthwise before slicing to get small enough slices. Slices from a butt are likely to come out in several different shapes; just be certain each slice is thin. Set aside.

2.   Combine the wine, hoisin sauce, soy sauce, sugar, ginger, and ¼ cup honey in a bowl. Add the pork slices, mix, and rub the marinade well into the meat. Cover and refrigerate 8 hours or overnight.

3.   Prepare the Steamed Gold Coin Sandwich Buns. The buns may be prepared in advance; reheat by steaming 5 minutes.

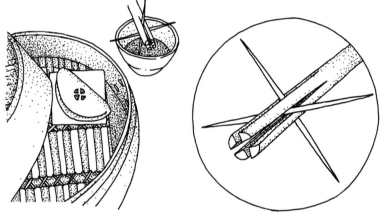

A delicate flower-like stamp is often used to decorate tea sandwiches and other steamed buns (see cover photo). Use a small, sharp knife to split an inexpensive wooden chopstick, making two 2- to 3-inch cuts at right angles to one another. Be careful; once it has penetrated the tip of the chopstick, the knife moves quickly. Insert toothpicks to spread the four quarters apart. Dip the tip of the chopstick into a small bowl of red food coloring and touch it lightly to the top of the bun before steaming.

4. Preheat the broiler. Line a cookie sheet with foil and set a large cooling rack on it. Lightly oil the rack. Combine the remaining ¼ cup of honey and the water in a small saucepan; heat gently, stirring until the honey dissolves. Lay the pork slices on the rack in a single layer. Brush them with the honey glaze. Set the baking sheet about 4 inches from the broiler and broil for 3 to 5 minutes or until the meat is seared. Turn the slices over, brush with honey glaze, and broil 3 to 5 minutes.

5. To serve, open each steamed sandwich bun and insert a slice or two of pork and a few green onion slivers. Serve hot or at room temperature.

NOTE The Chinese prefer pork butt, the fattier cut of meat, for this recipe, but a boneless pork loin is also very good. I do not use saltpeter, which is often used in barbecued meat recipes to bring out the reddish color.

STEAMED GOLD COIN SANDWICH BUNS

These steamed buns are traditionally stuffed with small slices of marinated pork, which approximate the size and color of gold coins.

Makes 24 buns

>   *1 envelope (2 teaspoons) active dry yeast*
>   *6 tablespoons sugar*
>   *¼ cup warm water (100 to 110°)*
>   *3½ cups all-purpose flour, plus more for kneading*
>   *1 cup warm milk (100 to 110°)*
>   *2 teaspoons double-acting baking powder*
>   *Asian sesame oil or vegetable oil*

1. Place the yeast and 1 tablespoon of the sugar in a small bowl. Add the warm water, stir, and let the mixture stand for 5 minutes to dissolve the yeast. It should foam and bubble. If it does not, discard and use a fresh package of yeast.

2. Put the flour and the remaining sugar in the work bowl of a food processor fitted with a metal blade. Process for 2 seconds. Combine the yeast mixture with the warm milk and, while the machine is running, pour the mixture down the feed tube in a steady stream. Process until the dough forms a rough ball. If the ball is sticky and wet, add more flour, a teaspoon at a time, and process a few seconds longer until the dough pulls away from the sides of the bowl. Remove the dough to a lightly floured board.

3. Knead the dough, dusting with flour as needed to keep it from sticking, until it is smooth and elastic, about 2 minutes. Form the dough into a ball and put it into a large, lightly oiled mixing bowl. Cover and set in a warm spot until the dough doubles in volume, about 1 hour.

4. Punch down the dough and turn it out on a lightly floured surface. Flatten it and put the baking powder in the center. Fold the edges of the dough over the baking powder. Knead until the baking powder is thoroughly incorporated. Invert the mixing bowl over the dough and let it rest for 10 minutes.

5. Divide the dough in half. Cover one half. Roll the other half into a 12-inch log; cut it into 12 pieces. Remove one piece and cover the rest. Roll the piece of dough into a flat 3½-inch circle. Lightly brush one half with oil; fold the unoiled side over the oiled one. Press together lightly. Set on a 3-inch square of parchment paper and place in a steaming basket. (You will need two baskets or you will need to steam two separate batches.) Repeat with the remaining dough; leave space between the buns in the baskets. Let the buns rise for 30 minutes or until they almost double in size, then steam them over boiling water for 15 minutes. When done, let them cool for a minute before serving.

SHRIMP-STUFFED EGGPLANT SANDWICHES (*China*)

Slices of eggplant are the "bread" in these crusty, succulent appetizers, surrounding a typical Chinese filling of shrimp mousse and sausage or ham. A coating of panko bread crumbs gives an extra crunch. Eggplant is native to Southeast Asia and is now grown in China as well. The Asian varieties available in American supermarkets are long and slender, and range in color from lavender to deep purple (almost black). They are seldom bitter and the skins are not tough; therefore, they do not require salting or peeling.

Serves 4

½ pound shrimp, shelled and deveined
1¼ teaspoons salt
1 green onion (including top), minced
½ teaspoon grated ginger
1 teaspoon Shao Hsing wine or dry sherry
½ teaspoon cornstarch
1 Chinese sausage (lop cheong), *coarsely chopped*
*   or 2 tablespoons minced Smithfield ham*
2 Asian eggplants, about 2 inches thick
½ cup flour
2 eggs
Salt and pepper, to taste
1 cup panko (*Japanese bread crumbs*) *or bread*
*   crumbs*
½ cup peanut oil, or more if needed

1.   Toss the shrimp with 1 teaspoon of the salt and let them sit for 10 minutes. Rinse with cold water, drain thoroughly, and blot dry. Coarsely chop the shrimp and transfer them to a bowl. Add ¼ teaspoon of salt, the green onion, ginger, wine, cornstarch, and Chinese sausage. Mix well. Set aside.

2.   Cut the eggplants crosswise into ⅓-inch-thick slices. For each sandwich, spread 1 tablespoon of the shrimp mixture on one slice and cover with another slice. Beat the eggs with a pinch of salt and pepper. Lightly dredge the sandwiches in flour, then dip them into beaten egg to coat them and roll them in the bread crumbs. Cover and refrigerate for an hour.

3.   Heat a large skillet and pour in 4 tablespoons of oil or enough to cover the bottom by about ¼ inch. When the oil is hot, arrange the eggplant sandwiches in the skillet and pan-fry for 3 to 4 minutes or until lightly browned. Turn them over to brown the other side. Remove from the pan; drain on paper towels. Serve immediately. If your skillet is not large enough to hold all the sandwiches, fry in batches, adding oil as needed.

CHA SIU BAO
Baked Barbecued Pork Buns
(China)

These buns are the ultimate Chinese snack food, eaten in China for breakfast, lunch, or between meals. Although they are most often served steamed, they are equally delicious baked. Cantonese barbecued pork can be bought in a Chinese delicatessen or you can make your own (see page 108).

Makes 20

> *1 recipe Chinese Sweet Bread Dough (page 47)*
> *1 teaspoon grated ginger*
> *1 tablespoon oyster sauce*
> *1 tablespoon hoisin sauce*
> *1 tablespoon dark soy sauce*
> *2 tablespoons plus 1 teaspoon sugar*
> *¾ cup plus 2 tablespoons water*
> *1 tablespoon peanut or corn oil*
> *1 cup finely chopped onion*
> *3 cups Cantonese barbecued pork, in ½-inch dice*
>   *(about 1 pound)*
> *1 tablespoon cornstarch dissolved in*
>   *1 tablespoon water*
> *1 teaspoon Asian sesame oil*
> *20 3-inch squares parchment paper*
> *2 egg yolks*

1. Prepare the Chinese sweet bread dough. Mix the ginger, oyster sauce, hoisin sauce, soy sauce, 2 tablespoons of sugar, and ¾ cup of water in a bowl.

2. Preheat a wok over medium-high heat. When hot, add the oil. When the oil is hot, add the onion and stir-fry until it is soft and translucent (do not brown). Add the pork and stir-fry for 30 seconds. Pour in the sauce mixture; mix and bring to a boil. Stir in the cornstarch mixture and cook until thick, about 15 seconds. Fold in the sesame oil. Remove to a bowl and refrigerate for 1 hour or until thoroughly chilled.

3. Cut the bread dough in half. On a floured board form each half into a 12-inch log; cut each log into 10 pieces. Roll out each piece into a 4-inch circle. Roll the outer 1 inch of each circle to about ⅛ inch thick; leave the middle slightly thicker.

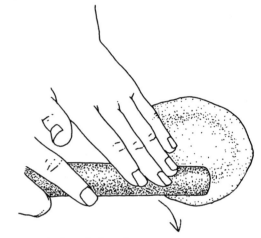

Rolling out a circle of dough

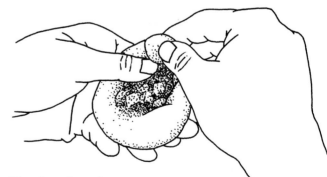

Pleating the edge

4. If right-handed, place a dough circle in the palm of your left hand. Put a heaping tablespoon of pork mixture in the middle, and lay your left thumb over it. With your right hand, bring up the edge of the dough and make a pleat in it. Rotate the circle a little and make a second pleat. As you make each pleat, gently pull it up and around as if to enclose the thumb. Continue rotating and pleating the edge, pinching the pleats together as you go. When the entire edge is pleated, remove your thumb; gather the tops of the pleats together and gently twist them into a spiral. Pinch to seal. Place the bun pleated side down on a parchment square. Repeat with the remaining dough and filling. Arrange the buns about 1½ inches apart on a baking sheet and let them rise until double in size, 30 minutes to 1 hour.

5. Preheat the oven to 350°. Beat the egg yolks with the remaining water and sugar. Brush the buns with the mixture. Bake 20 minutes. Serve warm.

CHINESE SWEET BREAD DOUGH

Chinese bread is quite sweet compared to Western breads, and it gets sweeter the further south you go in China. Most Chinese breads are steamed, which is why they look uncooked to the Western eye. This is the dough I use to make baked barbecued pork buns (page 46). Extra buns freeze well; to reheat them, take them straight from the freezer and bake at 350° for 5 minutes.

Makes enough for 20 barbecued pork buns

1 envelope (2 teaspoons) active dry yeast
3 tablespoons sugar
1 cup warm milk (100 to 110°)
1 egg
⅓ cup vegetable oil
3½ cups all-purpose flour, plus more for kneading

1. Put the yeast and 1 tablespoon of sugar in a small bowl. Add ¼ cup of warm milk. Let stand for 5 minutes, then stir to dissolve the yeast. It should foam and bubble. If it does not, discard and use a fresh package of yeast. Stir in the egg, oil, and remaining milk.

2. Put the flour and remaining sugar in the work bowl of a food processor fitted with a metal blade. Process for 2 seconds. With the machine running, pour the warm milk mixture down the feed tube in a steady stream. Process until the dough forms a rough ball. If the ball is sticky and wet, add a little more flour. Process a few seconds longer or until the dough pulls away from the sides of the bowl. Remove the dough to a lightly floured board.

3. Knead the dough, dusting as needed with flour to keep it from sticking, until smooth and elastic, about 2 minutes. Place it in a large oiled bowl, cover with plastic wrap, and let rise in a warm spot until doubled, about 1 hour. Punch the dough down and place it on a lightly floured surface. It is now ready to form into rolls, buns, or loaves.

SESAME CHICKEN CAKES
(Korea)

Serve this savory appetizer over a salad of dandelion leaves, chicory, or watercress as a simple first course. The crunchy texture and bitter flavor of the greens make a nice contrast to the soft and savory chicken cakes.

Makes 12 (serves 6)

DIPPING SAUCE
1 clove garlic, pressed through a garlic press
1 teaspoon sugar
1 tablespoon Asian sesame oil
2 tablespoons white vinegar
4 tablespoons Japanese-style soy sauce
1 teaspoon toasted sesame seeds
1 green onion (including top), thinly sliced

❀

1 pound ground chicken (mixed dark and light meat)
1½ tablespoons toasted sesame seeds
1 green onion (including top), thinly sliced
1 tablespoon grated ginger
⅛ teaspoon freshly ground black pepper
¼ teaspoon cayenne pepper
1 tablespoon Japanese-style soy sauce
1 teaspoon Asian sesame oil
3 tablespoons vegetable oil
1 bunch watercress, chicory, or dandelion greens, or a mixture

1.   Whisk together all the dipping sauce ingredients except the sesame seeds and green onions. Pour the mixture into a small bowl; stir in the sesame seeds and green onions. Set aside.

2.   In a medium bowl, mix together the chicken, sesame seeds, green onion, ginger, black and cayenne peppers, soy sauce, and sesame oil. Form the mixture into twelve 2-inch-diameter round, flat cakes.

3.   Preheat a large skillet over medium-high heat and add 1½ tablespoons of vegetable oil. When hot, add half the chicken cakes in a single layer; they should not touch each other. Fry until browned, 1 to 1½ minutes. Turn the cakes over and brown the other side, about a minute longer. Add a little more oil if necessary and cook the remaining cakes. Serve hot over the greens, with dipping sauce on the side.

LUMPIA UBOD
Hearts of Palm Spring Rolls
(Philippines)

Variations abound on lumpia, the Filipino version of the Chinese spring roll. This is a "fresh" spring roll, meaning that the roll is not deep-fried; instead, a cooked filling is wrapped in a lettuce leaf, and a fresh spring roll skin is wrapped around the lettuce and filling like a burrito.

The *ubod* in Lumpia Ubod is hearts of palm, a luxurious ingredient to Asians as well as Americans. Canned hearts of palm are available in Asian and gourmet markets; or you may substitute shredded snow peas, jicama, or bamboo shoots for a similar crunchy texture.

Makes 12 rolls

> 12 *lumpia wrappers (page 51)*
> 1/2 *pound medium shrimp, shelled and deveined*
> 1 *teaspoon salt*
> 1 *whole chicken breast, poached or steamed*

LUMPIA SAUCE
1 cup chicken stock
4 tablespoons brown sugar
1/4 teaspoon salt
3 cloves garlic
2 tablespoons dark soy sauce
1/2 tablespoon cornstarch
❀
2 tablespoons vegetable oil
2 large cloves garlic, chopped
1 onion, chopped
1 medium carrot, finely julienned
2 cups finely shredded cabbage
Salt and black pepper to taste
2 cups julienned hearts of palm
12 lettuce leaves

1.   Have the fresh lumpia wrappers ready at room temperature.

2.   Toss the shrimp with salt; let them stand for 10 minutes. Rinse with cold water, drain, and pat dry. Cut the shrimp into pea-sized pieces; set aside. Skin and bone the chicken and cut the meat into matchstick strips; set aside.

3.   Combine all the sauce ingredients except the cornstarch in a saucepan. Bring to a boil, reduce the heat to medium, and cook, stirring continuously, until the liquid reduces by one-fourth. Dissolve the cornstarch in 2 tablespoons of water and add it to the sauce. Cook until the sauce is thick enough to lightly coat a spoon. Keep warm.

4.   Preheat a large skillet or wok over medium-high heat. Add the oil, garlic, and onion; saute until the onion is soft and translucent. Add the shrimp; saute until they turn bright orange and separate into pieces. Add the chicken, carrots, and cabbage; stir-fry until the vegetables are tender but crisp, 1 to 2 minutes. Season to taste with salt and pepper. Fold in the hearts of palm and cook just to heat them, about 10 seconds.

5.   To serve, place a lettuce leaf on top of a lumpia wrapper. Drain the excess liquid from the filling. Spoon 2 to 3 tablespoons of filling on the lettuce. Roll up and fold in one end. Pour a little sauce over the top.

LUMPIA WRAPPERS

Two versions of lumpia wrappers may be purchased fresh or frozen in Asian markets. One is a round, paper-thin wrapper made of flour and water, which may be used for both fresh and fried lumpia. The slightly thicker, square wrappers (sometimes labeled spring roll wrappers) are made from flour, egg, and water, and are mostly used for fried lumpia. Here is a homemade, eggless version for fresh lumpia.

Makes 12 8-inch wrappers

1 cup all-purpose flour
1 cup cold water
Pinch of salt
Vegetable oil

1.   Combine the flour, water, and salt in a bowl and stir until thoroughly smooth. The batter should have the consistency of heavy cream.

2.   Set an 8-inch nonstick skillet or well-seasoned crepe pan over moderate heat. Lightly oil the surface; wipe off the excess oil with a paper towel. Dip a natural-bristle pastry brush into the batter and paint the bottom of the pan with overlapping strokes of batter. Cook until the wrapper begins to curl away from the edge, about 30 seconds. Peel and lift the wrapper from the pan and set it on a plate or a sheet of foil. Continue making wrappers in the same manner, oiling the pan lightly each time with a paper towel dipped in oil. The wrappers can be made up to a few hours ahead and kept at room temperature.

TONKATSU FINGERS
(Japan)

Tonkatsu is a Japanese adaptation of the Western pork cutlet, served with a commercially prepared peppered sauce containing ketchup and Worcestershire sauce. Cut into "finger" cutlets, it makes a delicious appetizer.

Serves 8 with other appetizers

4 boneless pork loin chops (½ inch thick)
¼ cup flour
Salt and freshly ground pepper, to taste
2 large eggs, beaten
2 cups panko (Japanese bread crumbs) or bread crumbs
Peanut oil for deep-frying
Lemon wedges, for garnish
Bottled tonkatsu sauce, to taste

1.   Slice the pork into ½-inch by 2½-inch strips. Season the flour with salt and pepper. Lightly dredge the pork strips with flour. Dip the strips into the beaten eggs, then coat each strip well with panko.

2.   Preheat a wok over medium-high heat. Add oil to a depth of 2 inches and heat it to 375°. Add a few pork strips at a time to the hot oil (don't crowd them). Deep-fry until golden brown, about 3 minutes. Drain on paper towels. Arrange on a serving plate garnished with lemon wedges and a dipping bowl of tonkatsu sauce.

COLD APPETIZERS AND SALADS

Pomelo and Chicken Salad
(recipe, pg. 61)

MA-HO
Galloping Horses
(Thailand)

Ma-Ho is a tantalizing snack that exemplifies the Thai flair for color, zesty flavors, and lightness. The pork, peanut, and mint topping is typically Thai—at once sweet, savory, and spicy. Pineapple slices provide a refreshing tart fruit backdrop. This easy-to-prepare dish is best when made in advance.

Makes 24 pieces

> 1 bunch fresh coriander
> 1 teaspoon black peppercorns
> 2 tablespoons chopped garlic (about 4 cloves)
> 12 ounces pork butt, finely chopped
> 2 tablespoons vegetable oil
> 2 tablespoons finely chopped shallots
> 1 fresh serrano chile, chopped
> 4 tablespoons roasted peanuts, coarsely
>   chopped or pounded
> 1½ tablespoons Thai fish sauce (nam pla)
> 2 tablespoons palm sugar or dark brown sugar
> 1 teaspoon lime juice
> 6 fresh mint leaves, chopped
> 1 pineapple
> Red chile slivers, for garnish

1.   Keep the fresh coriander in a bunch and submerge it in a basin of cold water to rinse off the sand between the roots and stems. Spin it in a lettuce spinner. Cut off and chop 1 tablespoon of the roots; set aside. Chop enough of the leaves to yield 2 tablespoons; leave the remaining leaves whole. Set aside.

2.   In a mortar, pound the peppercorns into a fine powder; add the coriander roots and garlic and pound together into a paste. If you prefer, you can finely chop the mixture in a mini-chopper.

3.   Preheat a well-seasoned wok over medium-high heat. Saute the pork without oil, breaking up the clumps, until browned and dry (about 3 minutes). The meat should look like dry grains. Remove and set aside.

4.   Reheat the wok and add the oil, peppercorn mixture, shallots, and chile; saute until the shallots are browned, 1 to 2 minutes. Return the pork to the wok and add the peanuts, fish sauce, and palm sugar; stir-fry until the mixture is browned and sticky, about 1 minute. Stir in the lime juice and remove the mixture to a plate. When the mixture has cooled, mix in the chopped mint and chopped coriander leaves.

5.   Peel the pineapple and cut it into ⅜-inch-thick slices. Cut the slices into 2-inch squares or triangles. Spoon a teaspoon of pork mixture onto each pineapple slice. Garnish with a coriander leaf and a red chile sliver. Cover and chill until ready to serve.

CANTONESE CHICKEN SALAD WITH CASHEWS
(China)

This salad is made with a whole roast chicken, bought at a Chinese delicatessen. When buying the chicken, ask for the roasting juices; they will be poured out of the bird's cavity into a take-out container for you. Be sure that the chicken is left whole; you'll need the delicious paper-thin roasted skin as well as the meat. Shredding the meat by hand gives a far better texture than cutting it up with a knife.

Serves 6

2 cups peanut or vegetable oil
2 ounces rice stick noodles
1 tablespoon dry Colman's mustard
1½ tablespoons water
Large pinch each sugar and salt
1 Cantonese-style roast chicken, left whole,
    plus juices
2 teaspoons soy sauce
1 tablespoon vinegar
1 teaspoon Asian sesame oil
4 green onions, mostly white section, cut into
    2-inch-long fine shreds
Leaves from 1 bunch fresh coriander
2 tablespoons toasted sesame seeds
5 to 6 cups shredded iceberg or romaine lettuce
1 cup roasted cashews

1. In a wok or small saucepan heat the oil to 375°. Pull the noodles apart into 4 small batches. Add one batch to the hot oil. The noodles should puff within a few seconds. If they do not, the oil is not hot enough. Remove the puffed noodles with chopsticks or tongs; drain them on paper towels. Repeat with the remaining noodles. When all the noodles are cooked, lightly crumble them. You should have about 4 cups.

2. Combine the mustard, water, sugar, and salt in a small bowl; blend thoroughly, then cover the bowl and allow it to sit for 10 minutes.

3. Open the cavity of the roast chicken and pour out any remaining juices; add them to the juices that came with the chicken. Strain the juices and skim off and discard any fat on the top. Mix 4 tablespoons of strained juices with the soy sauce, vinegar, and sesame oil; blend thoroughly and set aside.

4. Skin the chicken, then remove the meat from the bones. Hand-shred the meat into 2-inch-long by ¼-inch-wide shreds. Cut the skin into 2-inch-long thin slivers and toss it with the meat shreds. Set aside.

5. Mix the mustard mixture with the chicken in a large bowl. Add the chicken juices; mix. Add the green onions, coriander, and sesame seeds; toss together like a salad. Just before serving, add the lettuce and cashews; toss the salad and arrange it over a bed of crumbled rice stick noodles. Serve at room temperature.

STOVE-TOP GRILLED SHRIMP AND PAPAYA SALAD
(Thailand)

I learned stove-top grilling from two Thai chefs: Somchai Aksomboon, owner of the Siam Cuisine restaurant in Berkeley, California; and the executive chef at the renowned Oriental Hotel in Bangkok, whom I have never known under any other name than Chef Miki. It is a simple and clean technique for producing a delicious charred flavor without having to start up or clean the grill.

Serves 6 to 8

>   *1 pound medium shrimp (36 to 40 per pound)*
>   *2 teaspoons salt*
>   *1 tablespoon vegetable oil*
>   *1 large papaya*
>   *2 tablespoons Thai fish sauce (nam pla)*
>   *4 to 5 tablespoons fresh lime juice*
>   *(about 3 limes)*
>   *2 teaspoons sugar, or to taste*
>   *3 shallots, thinly sliced*
>   *2 stalks fresh lemongrass, white tender part only,*
>   *trimmed and sliced as thinly as possible*
>   *2 sprigs fresh mint leaves, coarsely chopped*
>   *1 tablespoon coarsely chopped fresh*
>   *coriander leaves*
>   *2 small red chiles, finely chopped*
>   *1 head red leaf lettuce, leaves washed*
>   *and patted dry*
>   *2 tablespoons roasted peanuts, coarsely*
>   *chopped or pounded*

1.   Shell and devein the shrimp. Toss them with the salt and let them stand for 10 minutes. Rinse with cold water, drain, and thoroughly pat dry.

2.   Cut a 12- by 18-inch sheet of heavy aluminum foil. Toss the shrimp with the oil. Lay the shrimp on one half of the foil, in no more than 2 layers. Fold the other half of the foil over the shrimp; fold the edges to seal the packet.

3.   Set a gas or electric burner on medium-high (if electric, allow it to preheat). Place the packet directly on the burner; it should puff up and begin to sizzle within seconds. If there is no sizzling sound, remove the packet and increase the heat, then return the packet to the burner. "Grill" the shrimp for 1 minute. Turn the packet over and grill 1 minute longer. Check for doneness by pressing down on the packet; if the shrimp feel firm to the touch, they are cooked. Open the packet and check. The shrimp should be firm and bright orange. Set aside to cool.

4.   Peel and seed the papaya; cut half of it into 1-inch cubes. Cut the rest into long, thin slices. Set aside.

5.   Combine the fish sauce, lime juice, sugar, shallots, lemongrass, mint, coriander, and chiles. Pour the mixture over the cooled shrimp; toss to mix. Mix in the papaya cubes.

6.   Shred half the lettuce leaves. Arrange the whole leaves around the edges of a platter and the shredded leaves in the middle. Top with the shrimp-papaya salad. Arrange the slices of papaya around the salad, and sprinkle the peanuts on top. Serve chilled.

SHRIMP AND SCALLOPS IN COCONUT-LIME SAUCE
(Thailand)

This Thai-style ceviche was inspired by the Lemongrass Restaurant in Bangkok. I saw owner Vorachoon Yuichinda and Chef Narin Chotipanang demonstrate it at a symposium on Thai cooking in 1989. Believe it or not, in the Lemongrass Restaurant kitchen it's made in a microwave. My version contains both shrimp and scallops. Serve it with decorative toothpicks.

Serves 4

> ½ pound large shrimp (about 26 to 30 per pound)
> 2 teaspoons salt
> ½ pound bay scallops
> 2¼ teaspoons sugar
> 5 tablespoons lime juice
> 6 tablespoons coconut cream
> 3 shallots, thinly sliced
> 2 Thai chiles (1 red, 1 green), coarsely chopped
> 1 tablespoon coarsely chopped fresh
>   coriander leaves

1.   Shell and devein the shrimp. Toss them with 1 teaspoon of the salt and let them sit for 10 minutes. Rinse thoroughly with cold water, drain, and pat dry.

2.   Toss the shrimp and scallops with the sugar, lime juice, and remaining salt in a bowl. Set aside to marinate for 10 minutes.

3.   Arrange the shrimp in its marinade in a single layer on a heatproof (or microwave-safe) glass or ceramic plate. Pour the coconut cream over them. Microwave on high for 2 minutes or steam (see page 13) for 5 minutes, or until the shrimp are bright orange and firm. Garnish with shallots, chiles, and coriander. Serve warm or chilled.

ASPARAGUS WITH SESAME-MISO DRESSING
(Japan)

Miso is a Japanese-style fermented bean paste. Aka, red miso, has a hearty, savory flavor. Mixed with toasted sesame seeds, it becomes a basic Japanese dressing. This simple salad can be served either at room temperature or chilled.

Serves 6

> 1 pound fresh asparagus tips, cut into 3-inch
>   lengths
> 3 tablespoons white sesame seeds
> 2 tablespoons sugar
> 4 tablespoons red miso
> 2 tablespoons mirin

1.   Blanch the asparagus in salted boiling water for about 2 to 3 minutes or until tender but still crisp. Drain, shower with cold water, and blot dry.

2.   Toast the sesame seeds in an ungreased skillet over medium heat until golden brown, about 3 minutes. Pour the seeds into a suribachi (Japanese grinding bowl) or mortar; crush and grind them into a paste. Add the sugar, which helps the grinding. Mix in the miso and mirin. The resulting dressing will be grainy and coarse. Gently fold the dressing into the asparagus until they are well coated. Serve mounded in individual dishes, Japanese style.

VARIATION This dressing also makes a great crudités-style dip. Place it in a small bowl and surround it with your choice of raw or cooked vegetables, such as asparagus, green beans, cucumber, or cauliflower.

Shrimp and Scallops in Coconut-Lime Sauce

YAM TUA POO
Winged Bean Salad
(Thailand)

In Thailand there is a green bean that has four-sided pods with serrated ridges that look like wings. Sometimes it appears in local Asian markets; however, the American green bean is an excellent substitute. In this colorful salad, the beans are combined with shrimp, chicken, coconut, and chile.

Serves 6

> 2 tablespoons dried shrimp
> 3 tablespoons grated unsweetened coconut
> 10 ounces winged beans or green beans
> 4 ounces small cooked and peeled shrimp
> 1 cup coarsely chopped cooked chicken
> 2 fresh serrano chiles (1 red, 1 green), chopped
> 2 tablespoons Crisp Fried Shallot Flakes (page 26)
> 2 tablespoons Crisp Fried Garlic Flakes (page 26)
> 3 tablespoons dry-roasted peanuts, chopped

DRESSING
> 1 tablespoon roasted chili paste (nam prik pao, see Note)
> 3 tablespoons lime juice
> 2 teaspoons sugar, or to taste
> 1½ tablespoons Thai fish sauce (nam pla)
> ¼ cup coconut cream

1.   Cover the dried shrimp with warm water for 20 minutes. Drain, coarsely chop, and set aside.

2.   Toast the grated coconut in an ungreased wok or skillet over medium heat, stirring until golden brown. Remove and set aside.

3.   Blanch the beans in boiling water until tender but still crisp. Cut them into diagonal ¼-inch-thick slices and put them in a large bowl. Cut the cooked shrimp into ¼-inch dice; add them to the beans. Add the chicken, dried shrimp, chile, half of the shallot and garlic flakes, and half of the peanuts. Toss to mix. Refrigerate.

4.   Mix all of the dressing ingredients together. Pour the dressing over the bean mixture; mix together thoroughly. Garnish the salad with the toasted coconut and the remaining shallots, garlic, and peanuts.

NOTE *Nam prik pao* is a "sweet-style" roasted chili paste, sometimes referred to as "chili jam." It contains pounded roasted shallots, garlic, and chiles. The paste is sweet-and-soured with palm sugar and tamarind. There is a delicious commercially prepared *nam prik pao* which I recommend and use. It is made by a company named Pantainorasingh and is labelled "chilli paste with soya bean oil."

YAM WOON SEN
Glass Noodle Salad
(Thailand)

Yam means salad in Thai. *Woon sen* is the Thai term for mung bean flour noodles. Mung bean noodles, popular in China and Thailand, are also packaged as bean thread, glass, transparent, or jelly noodles. This spicy noodle, chicken, and shrimp salad was originated by Executive Chef Miki of the Oriental Hotel in Bangkok; I have adapted it for the American kitchen.

Serves 6

4 ounces mung bean thread noodles
1 tablespoon vegetable oil
12 ounces ground chicken
Salt and pepper, to taste
4 serrano chiles (2 red, 2 green), seeded and
    chopped
6 tablespoons lime juice
4½ tablespoons Thai fish sauce (nam pla)
2 teaspoons sugar
⅓ cup thinly sliced shallots (about 4)
¼ cup fresh coriander leaves
½ pound cooked peeled shrimp
2 cups shredded lettuce
2 tablespoons Crisp Fried Shallot Flakes
    (page 26), for garnish

1. Cover the mung bean noodles with water until they are soft and pliable (about 10 minutes). Meanwhile, bring a large pot of water to a boil. Drain the noodles and add them to the pot. Reduce the heat to medium and cook until the noodles are plump and glass-like (about 3 to 5 minutes). Drain; shower the noodles with cold water and drain again. Refrigerate.

2. Preheat a wok or skillet and add the oil. When hot, add the chicken and saute, breaking it up into small morsels, until it turns white. Season to taste with salt and pepper. Remove from the pan; set aside to cool.

3. Mix together the chiles, lime juice, fish sauce, sugar, shallots, and coriander. Add the chicken, shrimp, and chilled noodles; mix well. Serve over a bed of shredded lettuce. Garnish with crisp fried shallots.

YAM SOM-O
Pomelo and Chicken Salad (Thailand)

One of the best tasting and most refreshing Thai chicken salads is made with pomelo. Sometimes spelled pummelo, this citrus fruit, indigenous to Thailand and Malaysia, looks like an oversized grapefruit that comes to a point at the top. It is eaten like a segmented orange rather than a grapefruit. California growers are now producing a quality pomelo that is as sweet and juicy as the ones I have tasted in Asia (though it's still less juicy and less acidic than a grapefruit). The pomelo, with its crisp, snappy texture, adds an exotic touch to tropical-style salads with vegetables, other fruits, and meats. Since it is seasonal (mid-November through January), sweet grapefruit makes a good substitute the rest of the year.

Serves 4 to 6

    1 whole chicken breast, poached or steamed
    1 pomelo or large grapefruit (sweet ruby red)
    1 or 2 red serrano chiles, chopped
    1 tablespoon Thai fish sauce (nam pla)
    1½ teaspoons sugar
    2 tablespoons fresh lime juice
    1 green onion, chopped
    1 tablespoon chopped fresh coriander
    1 tablespoon chopped fresh mint
    6 romaine lettuce leaves, shredded
    3 tablespoons chopped roasted peanuts
    2 tablespoons Crisp Fried Shallot Flakes (page 26)

1. Skin and bone the chicken breast. Hand-shred the meat into thin matchstick strips; set aside. Peel the pomelo or grapefruit and separate it into segments. Working over a bowl to catch any juices, peel away the membranes with your fingers or with a knife and gently flake the flesh apart into the bowl. Chill.

2.   Mix the chile, fish sauce, sugar, and lime juice together in a large bowl. Add the chicken, pomelo, green onion, coriander, and mint and toss together. Make a bed of shredded lettuce on a platter and arrange the salad on top; garnish with the peanuts and shallot flakes.

NUTA-AE
Sashimi Salad
(Japan)

Nuta-Ae, a miso-mustard-flavored sashimi salad, is a practical and delicious solution to leftover scraps of raw fish that are perfectly good but not quite suitable to serve as sashimi.

Serves 6 to 8

> *1 bunch green onions (including tops), cut into 2-*
> *inch lengths*
> *1 tablespoon Colman's dry mustard*
> *2 teaspoons water*
> *2 tablespoons saké (Japanese rice wine)*
> *1 tablespoon mirin (Japanese cooking rice wine)*
> *½ cup shiro miso (white soybean paste, see Note)*
> *2 tablespoons sugar*
> *3 tablespoons Japanese-style rice vinegar*
> *2 teaspoons Japanese-style soy sauce*
> *1 pound fresh sashimi-grade raw fish (such as*
> *tuna, albacore, or bass), cut into 1½-inch-*
> *long by ¼-inch-thick strips or ½-inch cubes*
> *1 tablespoon toasted sesame seeds, for garnish*

1.   Drop the green onions into boiling salted water for 10 seconds. Pat them dry and set aside. Mix the mustard and water into a smooth paste; let it stand to develop its flavor.

2.   Warm the saké and mirin together in a saucepan. Carefully ignite them with a match to burn off the alcohol. Add the miso and simmer over moderate heat until thick, about 2 minutes. Remove from the heat and let cool.

3.   Transfer the miso mixture to a bowl; blend in the mustard, sugar, vinegar, and soy sauce. Pour over the fish and toss to mix. Add the green onions. Arrange the salad on small individual saucers; garnish with sesame seeds. Serve chilled or at room temperature.

NOTE Miso, a Japanese staple, is a fermented soybean paste used for seasoning, pickling, salad dressings, marinades, and soup bases. It comes in a wide variety of flavors, textures, and colors. The three major types are red miso (*aka*), which has a strong, pungent flavor; the medium-colored type (*chu*), which has a mild taste; and white or tan miso (*shiro*), which has a light, mellow, slightly sweet taste. If miso is refrigerated in an airtight container it will keep for several months.

BON BON CHICKEN SALAD
(*China*)

Asian sesame paste is the basis for many Chinese salad dressings and sauces. It differs from tahini, its Middle Eastern counterpart, in that the seeds are toasted before being ground. Toasting enhances the color, fragrance, and flavor of the seeds and the paste made from them. Here sesame paste is combined with ginger, garlic, and chile oil to make a zesty dressing for a chicken breast and bean thread noodle salad. The name Bon Bon refers to the sound of whacking a cooked chicken breast with the side of a cleaver, the traditional way to break it apart into shreds.

Serves 8

> 2 *whole chicken breasts, poached (see page 71)*
> 2 *teaspoons Asian sesame oil*
> 2 *ounces mung bean thread noodles*

SICHUAN SESAME SEED DRESSING
1 *tablespoon peanut oil*
1 *teaspoon grated ginger*
1 *teaspoon finely minced garlic (about 2 cloves)*
3 *tablespoons Asian sesame paste*
3 *tablespoons soy sauce*
2 *tablespoons wine vinegar*
1 *tablespoon sugar*
1 *teaspoon Asian chile oil, or to taste*
3 *tablespoons (approximately) chicken stock,*
   reserved chicken poaching liquid, or water

✿

½ *English cucumber, peeled and cut into*
   matchstick pieces or 1½ cups blanched
   julienne green beans
2 *green onions, finely shredded*
1 *tablespoon toasted black or white sesame seeds*

1.   Poach the chicken with ginger and green onions as directed on page 71; reserve the poaching liquid. Remove the chicken meat from the bones; discard the skin and bones. With your fingers, tear the chicken into ¼-inch-wide shreds. Put them in a bowl with the sesame oil, toss to coat, and refrigerate.

2.   Cover the noodles with hot water until they are soft and pliable (about 10 minutes). Drain. Bring a large pot of water to a boil and add the noodles. Reduce the heat to medium; cook until the noodles are plump and glass-like, about 3 to 5 minutes. Pour the noodles into a colander, then plunge them into a bowl of cold water. Drain again and refrigerate.

3.   To make the dressing, heat the oil in a saucepan. When it is hot but not yet smoking, add the ginger and garlic. Cook until fragrant, then turn off the heat. Add the sesame paste, soy sauce, vinegar, sugar, and chile oil; blend thoroughly. Pour in enough reserved chicken poaching liquid to make a thin, creamy consistency. Chill.

4.   To assemble the salad, arrange the noodles on a serving platter with the cucumber or green bean pieces on top. Scatter the shredded chicken over the top. Pour the dressing over the salad. Garnish with the shredded green onions and sesame seeds. Serve chilled.

SWEET BEEF JERKY AND CASHEW SALAD
(Thailand)

A dish I ate at the Lemongrass Restaurant in Bangkok inspired this recipe. The salad is made with Chinese sweet beef or pork jerky, which comes packaged in plastic bags and is readily available in Asian markets.

Serves 4 to 6

> 1 stalk fresh lemongrass
> ½ cup julienne strips Chinese celery or regular celery (⅛ inch thick by 1½ inches long)
> 2 shallots, thinly sliced
> 1 green onion, including some of the top, thinly sliced
> 4 ounces Chinese beef or pork jerky, cut into ¼-inch by ¾-inch strips
> 1 tablespoon lime juice
> 1½ teaspoons Thai fish sauce (nam pla)
> 1 teaspoon sugar
> ¼ teaspoon dried chile flakes
> 8 fresh mint leaves, finely shredded
> ½ cup coarsely chopped fresh coriander leaves
> 1 cup unsalted cashews, toasted
> 6 lettuce leaves, for garnish

1.   Remove and discard the tough outer leaves of the lemongrass until a purple ring appears. Cut the tender white heart into very thin slices.

2.   Combine the celery, shallots, green onion, lemongrass, and beef jerky. Mix together the lime juice, fish sauce, sugar, and chile flakes; toss with the jerky mixture. Moments before serving, add the mint, coriander, and cashews and toss. Arrange the salad on a platter lined with lettuce leaves. Serve at room temperature.

HORENSO NO GOMA-AE
Spinach with Sesame Dressing
(Japan)

Toasted sesame seed dressing is a typical Japanese salad dressing. It is made from ground toasted sesame seeds flavored with soy sauce, sugar, rice vinegar, and saké. The dressing in this recipe is good with a variety of green vegetables, so don't hesitate to experiment.

Serves 4

> 1 large bunch fresh spinach
> 1 cup water
> 1 teaspoon salt
> 1 teaspoon toasted white sesame seeds, for garnish
> 1 teaspoon black sesame seeds, for garnish

GOMA (SESAME SEED) DRESSING
> 4 tablespoons white sesame seeds
> 2 tablespoons saké (Japanese rice wine)
> 2 teaspoons sugar
> 1 tablespoon Japanese-style soy sauce
> 1 teaspoon Japanese-style rice vinegar

1.   Keep the spinach in a bundle; wash it with cold water and drain thoroughly. Bring the water and salt to a boil in a wide saucepan. Lay the spinach in a flat bundle in the boiling water. Cook until the leaves are barely wilted (about 10 seconds). Remove the spinach from the pan and shower it with cold water to refresh it. Squeeze out the excess water. With the spinach still in a bundle, cut off and discard the large stems. Cut the bundle into 1½-inch lengths (do not unroll). Refrigerate.

2.   To prepare the Goma Dressing, toast the 4 tablespoons of sesame seeds in an ungreased skillet over medium heat, stirring occasionally, until golden brown, about 5 minutes.

Put the seeds into a *suribachi* (Japanese-style mortar), a regular mortar, or a mini-processor and grind them into a paste. Warm the saké in a small saucepan; ignite it to cook off the alcohol. Transfer the saké to a small bowl; blend in the sesame paste, sugar, soy sauce, and vinegar.

3.   Pour the sesame dressing over the spinach; mix gently. Divide the spinach among 4 bowls and serve at room temperature or chilled. Garnish with sesame seeds.

FRESH LOTUS ROOT SALAD (*China*)

Fresh lotus root is an intriguing rhizome which Asian cooks use as a vegetable. The root looks like a chain of sausages linked together in groups of three or four. Inside are a number of hollow canals. When the root is sliced crosswise, the canals produce an exotic, lacy pattern. In this recipe the lotus root, blanched briefly, remains crisp and refreshing.

Serves 8

> *1 pound fresh lotus root*
> *Boiling water*
> *¼ pound asparagus tips*
> *½ teaspoon grated ginger*
> *4 teaspoons sugar*
> *1½ tablespoons soy sauce*
> *2 tablespoons white vinegar*
> *1½ teaspoons Asian sesame oil*
> *1 tablespoon chopped fresh coriander*
> *Toasted black sesame seeds, for garnish*

1.   Rinse the lotus root with cold water. Trim and discard both ends. Peel the root with a vegetable peeler and slice it diagonally into ⅛-inch-thick slices. Plunge the slices into a bowl of acidulated water (about 2 teaspoons vinegar to 1 quart water); drain. Put the slices in a heatproof bowl and pour in enough boiling water to cover them; let sit for 5 minutes. Drain, rinse with cold water, and pat dry.

2.   Blanch the asparagus until tender but crisp. Refrigerate the asparagus and lotus root until chilled.

3.   Thoroughly combine the ginger, sugar, soy sauce, vinegar, sesame oil, and coriander in a bowl. Put the lotus root and asparagus in a shallow dish and pour the dressing on top. Arrange on individual salad plates; garnish with sesame seeds. Serve chilled.

NOTE Fresh lotus root appears in Asian markets in autumn. Select lotus roots as you do potatoes—look for hard, unblemished bulbs. Since lotus roots grow in muddy ponds, they are sometimes coated with a thin layer of mud, which rinses right off with cold water.

Fresh Lotus Root Salad

BARBECUED BEEF SALAD WRAPPED IN RICE PAPER
(*Vietnam*)

For a special treat, set out a "spring roll bar" at your next summer afternoon barbecue. All you need is a platter of vegetable garnishes, a grill for cooking the beef slices, and water bowls for moistening the rice paper wrappers. This "fresh" Vietnamese spring roll is not fried, which makes it lighter and very refreshing. The filling, though herbaceous and hearty, is also light. Note that the beef needs to be marinated for at least 3 hours before cooking.

Serves 6

> 1 pound boneless beef round (1 inch thick)
> 2 stalks fresh lemongrass (or 2 tablespoons dried lemongrass soaked in warm water for 1 hour)
> 2 shallots
> 3 cloves garlic
> 1 fresh serrano chile
> 1 tablespoon sugar
> 1 tablespoon Vietnamese fish sauce (nuoc mam)
> 1 tablespoon Asian sesame oil
> 1 tablespoon sesame seeds
> 2 ounces dried rice stick noodles
> Boiling water
> 12 large red lettuce leaves
> 1 small English cucumber, peeled and julienned
> 24 fresh mint leaves
> 36 fresh coriander leaves, each with a little stem
> Nuoc Cham Dipping Sauce (see Note)
> 12 12-inch dried rice paper circles

1. Cut the beef into 4-inch by ¾-inch pieces. Slice each piece across the grain into ¼-inch-thick strips.

2. Remove and discard the tough outer leaves of the lemongrass. Slice the tender white heart into 1-inch lengths and put them into a food processor with the shallots, garlic, chile, and sugar; process into a paste. Transfer the paste to a bowl and mix in the fish sauce, sesame oil, and sesame seeds. Add the beef slices, mix, and marinate for at least 3 hours or overnight.

3. In a medium bowl cover the rice stick noodles with boiling water; let stand 1 minute, then drain. Arrange the rice stick noodles, lettuce, cucumber strips, mint, and coriander in separate piles on a platter, leaving space for the beef. Refrigerate.

4. Just before serving, preheat a grilling rack over hot coals. Grill the beef strips for 30 seconds on each side, just until nicely seared. Or place the beef strips on the highest oven rack under a hot broiler and broil until seared on both sides. Arrange the beef on the platter.

5. Have a dish of dipping sauce and one or more wide bowls of warm water on the table. Each guest dips a rice paper circle into a water bowl and immediately spreads it flat on a dinner plate or a damp towel. The circle will rehydrate and become pliable in a few seconds. It is then ready to be filled and rolled.

6. To make a spring roll, lay a lettuce leaf on the bottom third of the moistened circle. Top it with 2 or 3 slices of beef, a large tablespoon of noodles, several strips of cucumber, and a few leaves of mint and coriander. Fold the near edge of the paper over the filling, then roll up the paper around the filling, keeping it taut. Halfway through, fold over one end to enclose the filling, then continue rolling, Dip the open end of the roll into the dipping sauce and eat it with your fingers.

NOTE To make Vietnamese Nuoc Cham Dipping Sauce, grind 4 garlic cloves, 2 fresh chiles (preferably serrano), and 2 tablespoons sugar into a paste in a mortar, blender, or mini-food processor. Stir in 6 tablespoons Vietnamese fish sauce (*nuoc mam*), 4 tablespoons fresh lime juice, and 6 to 8 tablespoons water. Strain into a dipping bowl.

TECHNIQUE NOTE It is possible to prepare a batch of rice paper circles ahead of time, but it is a bit tricky and requires many damp towels. Place a rice paper circle on a damp towel and brush the paper with warm water; cover it with another damp towel. (Keep the dry circles covered with a dry towel or the edges will curl up.) Moisten the circles one at a time; place each on top of the last damp towel and cover it with another damp towel, making a stack of alternating circles and towels. Do not allow the circles to touch while they are rehydrating or they will stick together. After they are softened (1 minute or longer), you can remove a few circles from the towels and stack them on the platter, or even fold them in half. Be careful not to tear them when pulling them apart.

CHICKEN AND CABBAGE SALAD
(*Vietnam*)

Think of this salad as a coleslaw with Vietnamese dressing. It goes very well with rice with Vietnamese "Spaghetti Sauce" (page 100) and Five-Spice Grilled Quail (page 120).

Serves 6 to 8

VIETNAMESE DRESSING
*1 or 2 fresh red serrano chiles, seeded and
    finely minced*
*2 small cloves garlic, finely minced or pressed
    through a garlic press*
1½ tablespoons sugar
2 tablespoons Vietnamese fish sauce (nuoc mam)
3 tablespoons fresh lime juice
2 tablespoons water

❀

1 small onion, thinly sliced
2 tablespoons white vinegar
1 whole chicken breast, steamed or poached
4 cups finely shredded cabbage
1 cup finely shredded carrot (about 1 carrot)
3 tablespoons finely shredded fresh mint leaves
Large handful fresh coriander sprigs, for garnish
Shrimp chips, for garnish (see page 27)

1. Stir together all the dressing ingredients until the sugar has dissolved. You should have about ½ cup. Set aside.

2. Toss the onion with the vinegar in a small bowl. Let it stand for 10 minutes, then drain.

3. Skin and bone the chicken breast. Hand-shred the meat into thin matchstick strips. In a large mixing bowl, toss together the chicken, cabbage, carrot, onions, mint, and dressing. Arrange the salad on plates. Top with fresh coriander leaves and garnish with shrimp chips.

TECHNIQUE NOTE The vegetables for this salad need to be cut into very thin julienne. A Japanese plastic mandoline does a wonderful job. It's especially good for hard vegetables, such as carrots; the julienne shreds come out perfectly even.

POACHED CHICKEN WITH TWO DIPPING SAUCES
(China)

Several recipes in this book called for poached and shredded chicken breasts. Whether you are poaching just breasts or a whole chicken with the head and feet, Chinese poaching produces the sweetest and purest taste in fresh young chicken. It is also incredibly simple. All you need is a large pot of boiling water with small chunks of crushed ginger and a few bruised green onions.

The customary method with a whole chicken is to plunge it into the boiling seasoned water; when the water reaches a second boil, the surface is skimmed of rising scum, then the pot is tightly covered and removed from the heat. The chicken cooks in the cooling liquid; therefore, the bird is subjected to minimal amounts of heat and the meat remains tender and juicy. It is essential to use the freshest chicken. Reserve the poaching liquid and use it in place of water when making chicken stock, or use as is as a thin stock.

Serves 8

> 3 1-inch chunks ginger, crushed
> 3 green onions, slapped with the side of a cleaver and tied in a knot
> 2 large whole chicken breasts
> 1 to 2 tablespoons Asian sesame oil

OYSTER-SESAME DIPPING SAUCE
2 tablespoons oyster sauce
1½ tablespoons chicken stock
1 teaspoon sugar
1 teaspoon Asian sesame oil

SEARED GINGER-GREEN ONION OIL
4 green onions (white part only), cut into 2-inch shreds
6 thin slices fresh ginger, cut into thin shreds
2 teaspoons salt
6 tablespoons peanut oil

❁

6 cooked baby bok choy, for garnish
Fresh coriander sprigs

1.   In a large heavy stockpot combine the ginger and green onions with enough water to cover the chicken breasts by 1 inch. (If you are not sure, have a kettle ready with more boiling water.) Bring to a boil and add the chicken breasts; add more boiling water if necessary to fully cover the chicken. Bring the water to a second boil, skim the surface clear of scum, cover the pot, and reduce the heat to low. Simmer for 10 minutes and turn off the heat. *Do not remove the lid* or the heat will dissipate. Allow the chicken to steep 40 minutes for a couple of breasts, 1 hour for a whole chicken.

2.   Remove the chicken from the poaching liquid. Rub the skin with sesame oil and refrigerate until chilled. Meanwhile, prepare one or both of the dipping sauces as follows. *For the Oyster-Sesame Sauce:* combine the ingredients and place in a dipping saucer. *For the Ginger-Green Onion Oil:* Scatter the green onions in a shallow heatproof saucer. Top with ginger and salt. Heat the oil; when hot, carefully pour it over the other ingredients (it will sizzle).

3.   Bone and split the chicken breasts, leaving the skin attached if desired, and cut diagonally into ½-inch-thick slices. Arrange the chicken on a platter with the baby bok choy. Serve with your choice of sauces, either in small bowls for dipping or drizzled over the chicken. Garnish with coriander sprigs.

NOODLES, DUMPLINGS, AND RICE DISHES

Savory Chicken and Rice in a Lotus Leaf
(recipe, pg. 102)

SEAFOOD AND NOODLES IN A CLAY POT
(*Thailand*)

I first tasted this dish in a Bangkok restaurant called the Seafood Supermarket. It started out as a supermarket selling fresh local seafood and produce. The owner set out a few tables and hired a cook. After customers bought their daily staples, they would pick out some fish or shellfish plus appropriate vegetables and send them to the cook. Five or ten minutes later, freshly cooked seafood dishes would be brought to their tables. The supermarket is now massive, with tables for about 100 served by cooks in an open kitchen packed with grills, broilers, and a dozen woks.

Serves 6 to 8

> 3 ounces dried bean thread noodles
> 1 small Dungeness crab or 3 or 4 blue crabs, preferably live
> ¼ pound medium shrimp (36 to 40 per pound)
> ½ pound large squid
> ½ teaspoon black peppercorns
> 1 tablespoon chopped fresh coriander root
> 4 cloves garlic
> 1 teaspoon sugar
> 1 tablespoon Golden Mountain sauce or dark soy sauce
> 1 tablespoon light soy sauce
> 2 teaspoons oyster sauce
> 1 tablespoon Shao Hsing wine or dry sherry
> 1 teaspoon Asian sesame oil
> 2 tablespoons vegetable oil
> 3 quarter-sized slices ginger, crushed
> 4 red chiles, chopped into ½-inch pieces
> 4 green onions, cut into 2-inch lengths
> 1 cup water, or more if needed
> ½ cup Thai sweet basil leaves
> Fresh coriander sprigs, for garnish

1. Soak the bean thread noodles in warm water until soft and pliable, about 10 minutes. Drain and set aside. If using a cooked crab, have the fishmonger crack it in large pieces. If using a live crab, kill, clean, and crack it as directed on page 41 and cut it into chunks. Shell and devein the shrimp; pat them dry. Clean the squid and cut them into 1-inch rings and tentacles (see Technique Note, page 86).

2. Grind the peppercorns in a mortar or spice mill. Add the coriander root and garlic and pound into a paste. In another bowl, combine the sugar, Golden Mountain sauce, soy sauce, oyster sauce, wine, and sesame oil.

3. Add the oil to a Chinese clay pot and set it over medium heat (or add the oil to a preheated wok). Add the pounded mixture and cook until fragrant. Increase the heat to high and add the ginger, chiles, and raw crab pieces; toss for a minute to brown slightly. Add the shrimp and green onions and stir-fry for 30 seconds. Add the soy sauce mixture and noodles; toss and mix together. Stir in the water, cover the pot, reduce the heat to medium, and braise for 8 minutes, stirring occasionally. Increase the heat to medium-high and stir in the squid. (If using cooked crab, add it at this point.) Top with the basil leaves, cover, and cook until the squid is done, about 3 minutes longer. If the mixture seems dry, add a little more boiling water. Bring the clay pot to the table, or if cooking in a wok, transfer to a serving dish. Garnish with coriander. Serve hot with rice and vegetables.

DAN-DAN MEIN
Cool Sesame Chicken Noodles (China)

Dan-Dan Mein has as many variations as "spaghetti sauce." The few essential ingredients that make up the Sichuan-style sauce are toasted sesame paste, garlic, ginger, and soy sauce, and the preserved Sichuan mustard which gives it a distinctive bite. The name refers to the sound made by the clappers of the street hawkers peddling their noodles.

Serves 6

> 1 pound thin fresh Chinese egg noodles
> 1 tablespoon Asian sesame oil
> 1 cup ground pork
> 3 tablespoons soy sauce
> 1 tablespoon sugar
> 2 tablespoons peanut oil
> 1 teaspoon grated ginger
> 2 teaspoons finely minced garlic
> 1-inch lump Sichuan preserved mustard greens, rinsed with cold water and finely chopped
> 3 tablespoons Chinese sesame paste or peanut butter
> 1 cup chicken stock
> ½ tablespoon red wine vinegar
> 1 tablespoon Asian hot chili oil, or to taste
> 4 tablespoons minced green onions, for garnish

1. Bring 4 quarts of salted water to a boil in a large pot. Gently pull the noodles apart and add them to the boiling water, stirring gently to separate the strands. Bring to a second boil and cook 1 minute longer. Pour the noodles into a colander, then turn them out into a bowl of cold water. Drain and rinse with cold running water to remove excess starch. Drain well, toss with the sesame oil, and divide among 6 individual bowls.

2. Combine the pork with 1 tablespoon of the soy sauce and 1 teaspoon of the sugar. Preheat the wok; when hot, add 1 tablespoon of the peanut oil. When the oil is hot, add the pork and stir-fry, breaking up any lumps into morsels, until the pork is fully cooked and dry, about 2 minutes. Remove and set aside.

3. Reduce the heat to medium and add the remaining peanut oil to the wok. Add the ginger, garlic, and Sichuan mustard and gently saute until browned, about 30 seconds. Add the sesame paste, the remaining soy sauce and sugar, and chicken stock and simmer together for a few minutes. Return the pork to the wok and stir in the vinegar and hot chili oil. Ladle the sauce on top of the noodles and garnish with green onions. Serve at room temperature.

VARIATION Cover ¼ cup tiny dried shrimp with 1 cup hot water for 10 minutes, drain, and mince. Stir-fry with the ginger, garlic, and mustard mixture in Step 3.

SHANGHAI-STYLE BRAISED NOODLES
(China)

The Shanghai noodle is fatter and rounder than other Chinese noodles. The extra thickness and density makes it perfect for a lightly braised noodle dish; the noodles absorb the flavors of the braising liquid without disintegrating the way thinner noodles might. Shanghai noodles are available in better Chinese markets.

Serves 4 to 6

1 pound fresh Shanghai-style noodles
12 ounces pork loin or boneless chicken breast

MARINADE
2 teaspoons soy sauce
2 teaspoons Shao Hsing wine or dry sherry
¼ teaspoon sugar
1 teaspoon cornstarch
½ teaspoon Asian sesame oil

❀

2 tablespoons peanut oil
2 cloves garlic, peeled and chopped
1 small carrot, cut into thin matchsticks
1½ cups shredded purple cabbage
    or 2 cups shredded Chinese tientsin cabbage
1 cup garlic chives, cut into 1½-inch lengths
    or 1 leek, cut into 1½-inch lengths,
    split lengthwise, and slivered
¾ cup chicken stock
2 tablespoons light soy sauce
1 tablespoon dark soy sauce or 1½ teaspoons
    oyster sauce
2 tablespoons Shao Hsing wine or dry sherry
½ teaspoon sugar
⅛ teaspoon ground white pepper
1 teaspoon Asian sesame oil

1.   Bring 4 quarts of salted water to a boil in a large pot. Gently pull the noodles apart and add them to the boiling water. Bring to a second boil and cook for 1 minute. Drain, rinse with cold water, and drain again.

2.   Cut the pork or chicken into ¼-inch shreds 1¼ inches long. Combine the meat with the marinade ingredients in a small bowl; set aside.

3.   Preheat a wok over medium-high heat. When hot, add the oil and garlic and cook until lightly browned, a few seconds. Add the meat and stir-fry until the shreds feel firm to the touch, about 45 seconds. If using chicken, remove it and set it aside; pork can stay in the wok. Add the carrot and cabbage and stir-fry for 45 seconds. Add the chives and stir-fry for 5 seconds longer. Remove the mixture to a bowl.

4.   Add the chicken stock, soy sauces, wine, sugar, pepper, and sesame oil to the wok. Bring to a boil, add the noodles, and simmer over medium-high heat until the noodles completely absorb the sauce, about 3 minutes. Return the meat and vegetables to the wok and toss to combine and reheat. Serve hot.

KOW SOI
Chiang Mai Curry Noodles (Thailand)

Creamy, rich, aromatic, spicy, and extremely satisfying, this is Thai comfort food. As with many Thai curry dishes, having the curry paste made ahead of time makes this entree quick and easy.

Serves 4

1 pound fresh Chinese egg noodles
2 tablespoons vegetable oil
3 cloves garlic, chopped
1 tablespoon Basic Red Curry Paste (page 18)
    or prepared red curry paste
½ cup coconut cream
½ pound chopped boneless chicken meat,
    preferably dark
½ cup medium coconut milk
2½ cups chicken stock
2 teaspoons Indian curry powder
½ teaspoon turmeric powder
3 tablespoons Thai fish sauce (nam pla)
1 teaspoon sugar
1 cup shredded cabbage
1½ teaspoons lemon juice
2 green onions, coarsely chopped
2 lemons, cut into wedges

1.   Bring 2 quarts of salted water to a boil. Add the noodles, stirring to separate the strands. Bring the water to a second boil and cook 45 seconds. Drain the noodles in a colander and rinse thoroughly with running cold water. Drain and shake off the excess water. Distribute the noodles among 4 small soup bowls.

2.   Heat the oil in a saucepan; add the garlic and gently saute until lightly browned. Add the curry paste and lightly saute for a minute. Increase the heat to medium-high; add the coconut cream and stir continuously until the cream reduces and becomes oily. Add the chicken; saute lightly, breaking up the lumps. Add the coconut milk, chicken stock, curry powder, turmeric, fish sauce, and sugar. Simmer for 5 minutes. Add the cabbage and cook 30 seconds longer. Add the lemon juice and pour the soup over the noodles. Top with chopped green onions and lemon wedges. Serve hot.

PHO
Hanoi Beef Soup with Rice Noodles (Vietnam)

Throughout Asia, snacks and light meals are typically enjoyed at any time of day. Besides being a wonderful first course, this Vietnamese soup, fragrant with star anise, can be eaten as breakfast, a quick lunch, or a light dinner.

Serves 8

> 2 1-inch chunks fresh ginger
> 3 shallots, unpeeled
> 1 onion, unpeeled
> 2½ quarts water
> 1½ pounds oxtails, chopped into sections
> 1 pound beef shanks
> 2 whole star anise
> 1 cinnamon stick
> 3 whole cloves
> ¼ cup Vietnamese fish sauce (nuoc mam)
> 1 teaspoon salt, or to taste
> ½ pound flat rice stick noodles, soaked in water
>   for 20 minutes
> 6 ounces beef flatiron steak, trimmed of fat
>   and sliced paper-thin
> 2 green onions, in 2-inch-long julienne strips
> 1 yellow onion, sliced very thin
> 2 cups bean sprouts
> ¼ cup coarsely chopped fresh coriander leaves
> 1 lime, sliced into 8 wedges
> 2 red chiles, thinly sliced

1.   Put the ginger, shallots, and onion on a baking sheet and set them under a hot broiler until charred.

2.   Combine the water, oxtails, and beef shanks in a stockpot and bring it to a boil. Thoroughly skim and discard the scum from the surface. Add the charred ingredients, star anise, cinnamon, and cloves. Reduce the heat to low and simmer for 2 hours. Remove the oxtails and reserve them for another use. Remove the meat from the shanks; shred the meat and reserve it. Return the shank bones to the simmering stock. Simmer 1 hour longer.

3.   Strain the stock, discard the bones, degrease the stock, and return it to the pot. Add the fish sauce and salt to taste and keep at a low simmer.

4.   Bring 3 quarts water to a boil in a separate pot. Drain the noodles, add them to the pot, and boil until tender, about 1 minute. Drain the noodles in a colander and divide them among 8 deep 1½- to 2-cup soup bowls. Top each bowl of noodles with shredded cooked beef, raw beef slices, green and yellow onions, and bean sprouts. Ladle about 1¼ cups hot stock into each bowl; this will cook the beef. Top with fresh coriander. Serve with a wedge of lime and chiles for seasoning each serving to taste.

STAR ANISE BEEF STEW WITH NOODLES
(China)

This aromatic stew is best cooked in a Chinese sandy clay pot, which gives it an earthy flavor metal pans cannot produce. If you do not have one, a small dutch oven will work as well. This is a somewhat simplified version, using common Western stewing cuts of beef. For a more village-style version, try Chinese stewing beef, which comes from the plate just below the rib. The Chinese would also include the cartilage and tendons, primarily for their textures. If you use them, cut them into 1½-inch pieces and simmer for about 2 hours or until not quite tender. Remove and add them to the braising beef and simmer together for the last hour.

Serves 6

> 2½ to 3 pounds beef stew meat
> 1½ tablespoons peanut oil
> 2 ½-inch chunks ginger
> 3 cloves garlic, peeled
> 3 whole green onions
> ¼ cup Shao Hsing wine or dry sherry
> ¼ cup each dark and light soy sauce
> 2 tablespoons rock sugar (see Note) or white sugar
> 4 to 6 whole star anise
> 2 pieces dried tangerine peel (optional)
> 1 cinnamon stick
> 2 cups (approximately) boiling water
> 2 carrots, peeled and cut into roll-cut pieces (see Note)
> 2 Chinese white radishes (daikon), peeled and cut into roll-cut pieces (about ½ pound)
> 1 pound Chinese egg noodles, cooked

1. Place the beef in a large stock pot and add cold water to cover. Bring to a boil, cook for 3 minutes, drain, and rinse. Cut the meat into 2-inch chunks.

2. Add the oil to a 2½- or 3½-quart sandy clay pot over medium heat. Add the ginger, garlic, and green onions and cook until they are lightly browned and fragrant. Increase the heat to medium-high, add the beef chunks, and brown them on all sides. Add the wine, soy sauces, rock sugar, star anise, tangerine peel, cinnamon, and boiling water to cover; stir to mix. Bring to a boil, reduce the heat, and simmer, stirring occasionally, until the meat is tender, 1½ to 2 hours depending on the cut of meat.

3. Remove the beef and set it aside. Strain the sauce and spoon off the excess fat. Return the sauce to the pot, add the carrots and radishes, and cook until the vegetables are tender, about 20 minutes. Return the beef to the sauce to reheat. Serve the stew over noodles.

NOTES Chinese rock sugar, large amber-colored crystals sold in Chinese markets, has a mellow, unrefined kind of sweetness that to me is not as cloying as other sugars. If you can't find it, use ordinary white sugar.

To make roll-cut pieces of carrots, daikon, and similarly shaped vegetables, slice at an angle, rolling the vegetable ¼ to ½ turn after each slice to produce wedge-shaped pieces of approximately the same size.

RED CURRY MUSSELS WITH NOODLES
(Thailand)

This dish is especially attractive with the large green-shelled mussels from New Zealand, the same species found all over Southeast Asia. The blue-black mussels more common around here are also fine. If you have the curry paste already made up, this recipe takes only about 20 minutes from start to finish.

Serves 6

> 1 14-ounce can unsweetened coconut milk
> 3 pounds fresh mussels (about 6 dozen)
> 1 to 2 tablespoons Basic Red Curry Paste
>   (page 18) or prepared red curry paste
> 1½ tablespoons Thai fish sauce (nam pla)
> 2 teaspoons palm sugar (see Note)
>   or brown sugar
> 1 teaspoon paprika
> 8 fresh or dried kaffir lime leaves
> 6 fresh red chiles
> 1 cup straw mushrooms, fresh or canned
> 1 large handful sweet basil leaves (horabha)
> 1 pound cooked flat Chinese-style egg noodles
>   or 6 cups steamed rice

1.   Skim off ½ cup of the "cream" from the coconut milk (see page 19) and set it aside in a bowl. Clean, scrub, and debeard the mussels.

2.   Heat a saucepan or wok over medium-high heat. Add the coconut cream and cook, stirring continuously, until the cream reduces and thickens and the oil separates around the edges. Add 1 tablespoon of the curry paste, the fish sauce, palm sugar, and paprika and cook, stirring continuously, until the sauce thickens and the flavor is fully developed, about 5 minutes. Add the remaining coconut milk, lime leaves, and chiles; bring to a boil, immediately reduce the heat to low, and simmer uncovered until slightly reduced, about 5 minutes. Taste for seasoning and add more curry paste if needed. Increase the heat to medium-high and add the mussels, mushrooms, and basil. Cook until the mussels open, 3 to 5 minutes. Transfer to a large serving bowl. Serve over noodles or hot rice.

NOTE Palm sugar tastes like a cross between caramel and maple sugar candy. It is made from the sap tapped from the Palmyra palm. In Southeast Asian cooking it is used for both sweet and savory dishes and marketed as jaggery and coconut sugar. You can substitute dark brown sugar, although it really doesn't come close in flavor.

SUB GUM CHOW MEIN
Noodle Pancakes with Meat and Vegetables
(China)

Sub gum means a variety or mixture, in this case of contrasting tastes and textures. Many of the ingredients can be replaced with comparable items or omitted.

Serves 4

1 recipe Shallow-Fried Noodle Pancakes (page 85)
6 dried Chinese black mushrooms

MARINADE
⅛ teaspoon sugar
1 tablespoon Shao Hsing wine or dry sherry
1 teaspoon cornstarch
½ teaspoon Asian sesame oil
❀
1 whole chicken breast, boned, cut into
 ¼-inch-thick slices
6 ounces medium shrimp, shelled and deveined
2 teaspoons salt
4 ounces barbecued pork or 2 Chinese sausages
2 to 4 tablespoons peanut or corn oil
2 quarter-sized slices fresh ginger, crushed
2 cloves garlic, peeled and minced
3 green onions, diagonally cut into 1-inch slices
8 fresh water chestnuts, peeled, cut into
 ¼-inch slices
1½ cups purple cabbage, cut into 1-inch cubes
1½ cups Chinese bok choy stems and leaves,
 cut diagonally into 1-inch pieces
¼ teaspoon white pepper
1 teaspoon sugar
2 tablespoons Chinese soy sauce

1 cup chicken stock
2 teaspoons cornstarch
1 to 2 teaspoons Asian sesame oil
Red wine vinegar, for seasoning

1.   Prepare the noodle pancakes as directed on page 85; keep them warm.

2.   Cover the mushrooms with warm water; soak until soft and pliable, about 20 minutes. Remove the mushrooms and discard the stems; slice caps into ¼-inch strips. Set aside.

3.   Combine the marinade ingredients in a small bowl, add the chicken, and toss together. Toss the shrimp with 1 teaspoon of the salt. Let them stand for 10 minutes, rinse well with cold water, and pat dry. Set aside. Cut the barbecued pork into julienne strips (or the sausage into diagonal slices); set aside.

4.   Preheat the wok; when hot, add 2 tablespoons of the oil. Add the chicken and stir-fry over medium-high heat until just slightly underdone, about 30 seconds. Add the shrimp and stir-fry until they curl and stiffen, about 30 seconds. Add the barbecued pork, toss to mix, and remove the meat to a bowl.

5.   Add the remaining oil to the wok and add the remaining salt, the ginger, garlic, and green onions; saute lightly until the garlic is browned. Add the mushrooms, water chestnuts, cabbage, and bok choy and stir-fry until the vegetables are cooked but still crisp, about 1½ minutes. Season with the white pepper, sugar, and soy sauce. Thoroughly blend the chicken stock with the cornstarch; pour it into the wok and stir immediately until thickened. Return the chicken mixture to the wok and add the sesame oil; toss to mix and heat. Serve over the noodle pancakes. Pass a shaker of vinegar at the table for seasoning individual portions to taste.

SHALLOW-FRIED NOODLE PANCAKES

A "pancake" of crisp-fried noodles (the real *chow mein*) can be a base for various stir-fried dishes. The current fashion ("Hong Kong style") is to use very thin fresh egg noodles and to fry them to a potato-chip crispness. I like a crisp outside, but I prefer to use a medium-width noodle, which produces a slightly chewy texture under the crunchy crust.

Serves 4

1 pound medium-width fresh Chinese egg noodles
4 to 6 tablespoons peanut oil
½ teaspoon salt

1.   Bring 2 quarts water to a boil in a large saucepan or stockpot. Remove the noodles from the bag and gently pull them apart to separate the strands. Add the noodles to the pot, stirring to separate them. Bring the pot to a second boil and cook 45 seconds longer. Drain the noodles, rinse them with cold water, and drain thoroughly.

2.   Heat a 10-inch skillet over medium-high heat. Add 2 tablespoons of the oil and sprinkle half the salt evenly in the pan. When hot, add half the cooked noodles, spreading them evenly over the bottom of the pan. Lightly pat the noodles to form a "pancake." Reduce the heat to medium-low and cook until the bottom forms a golden brown crust, 3 to 4 minutes. Add a little more oil if needed to prevent sticking. Turn the pancake over and brown the other side, 3 to 4 minutes longer. When slightly crisp, remove the noodles to a hot serving platter and keep in a warm oven. Repeat with the remaining noodles, salt, and oil.

CHAR KWAY TEOW
Stir-Fried Rice Noodles (Singapore)

Nothing is more fascinating and delicious than eating at the open-air street hawker centers in Asia, particularly in Singapore. Each stall serves a specialty, typically an honest, unpretentious, home-style dish for $1 to $3 a plate.

This rice noodle dish is hawker food at its best. If done right, its fragrance will tell you how good it's going to be as soon as it arrives at your table. Singapore hawkers will use whatever seafoods are available, including cockles and sliced fish cakes in addition to those suggested in this recipe. Feel free to experiment.

Serves 4 to 6

2 Chinese sausages (lop cheong)
¼ pound medium shrimp (36 to 40 per pound), shelled and deveined
1 teaspoon salt
¼ pound cleaned squid, with tentacles (see Technique Note)
¼ pound Chinese barbecued pork
¼ teaspoon white pepper
1½ tablespoons dark soy sauce
1½ tablespoons light soy sauce
1 tablespoon oyster sauce
2 pounds fresh rice noodles, in ⅝-inch-wide strips
4 tablespoons peanut oil
4 cloves garlic, chopped
4 shallots, sliced (½ cup sliced)
6 fresh red chiles, seeded and chopped
1 cup bean sprouts, tails removed
1 cup shredded Chinese cabbage
2 large eggs
4 green onions, chopped
Fresh coriander sprigs, for garnish

1.   Steam the sausages for 10 minutes (see page 13). Cut them in thin diagonal slices. Toss the shrimp with ½ teaspoon of the salt. Let them stand for 10 minutes, rinse well with cold water, drain, and pat dry. Cut the squid into ¼-inch rings and tentacles. Cut the barbecued pork into ¼-inch-thick slices. Combine the white pepper, soy sauces, and oyster sauce in a bowl; set aside.

2.   Just before cooking, put the noodles in a large bowl and pour boiling water over them. Stir gently with chopsticks to separate the strands, drain, and shake off the excess water.

3.   Preheat a wok; when hot, add 2 tablespoons of the oil. Add the remaining ½ teaspoon salt and the garlic, shallots, and chiles and cook over medium-high heat until the garlic is golden brown. Increase the heat to high and toss in the shrimp and squid; stir-fry until the shrimp turn bright orange and the squid looks opaque white, about 2 minutes. Add the sausage slices, barbecued pork, bean sprouts, and cabbage; toss and stir until the vegetables begin to wilt. Remove everything in the wok to a platter and set aside.

4.   Add the remaining 2 tablespoons of oil to the wok; when hot, toss in the well-drained noodles. Gently toss and flip the noodles to heat them through. Be careful not to break them; it is okay if they brown slightly. Push the noodles up the sides of the wok to make a well in the middle; pour in the soy sauce mixture, then toss the noodles gently to sauce them evenly. Make a well again and break the eggs into the middle. Without mixing them with the noodles, scramble the eggs lightly. When the eggs begin to set, add the green onions and return the seafood mixture. Gently toss together to reheat and mix. Serve hot, with a hot chili sauce for seasoning to taste. Garnish with coriander sprigs.

NOTE Both here and in Asia, fresh rice noodles are usually purchased rather than made at home. Look for them in Asian markets or Chinese take-out dim sum shops. This dish can be prepared with dried rice noodles; however, it is worth taking the time to seek out the fresh variety.

Make certain that your wok is well seasoned or the fragile rice noodles will break apart and stick to the pan. Although I hesitate recommending that you cook with a nonstick wok or skillet, they will work fine if you are more comfortable with them.

TECHNIQUE NOTE To clean squid, start by separating all the tentacles from the heads, cutting across as close as possible to the eyes. Squeeze out and discard the hard, pea-sized beak in the center of each cluster of tentacles. Rinse the tentacles and drain them in a colander.

Grasp the mantle (the saclike "body" of the squid) in one hand and the head in the other and pull apart; the entrails will pull out attached to the head. Pull the transparent quill out of each mantle. Discard everything but the tentacles and mantles. Running a little water into each mantle to open it up, reach in with a finger and pull out any entrails remaining inside. (Working over a second colander to catch all the debris will make cleanup easier.) You can remove the spotted outer skin or leave it on (I prefer to remove it). Transfer the cleaned mantles to a cutting board, slice them crosswise to the desired size, and add them to the tentacles in the colander. Give everything another rinse and drain thoroughly.

FUN GWAU
Steamed Translucent Dumplings (China)

These dumplings make great finger food for a cocktail party. They can be prepared and steamed in advance and reheated a few minutes before serving (refrigerate or freeze as directed in the introduction to Ha Gow, page 88). The wheat starch wrappers have an interesting, chewy texture, a unique translucent appearance, and the ability to absorb flavors. Roll out the wrappers as thin as possible, otherwise they can be rubbery.

Makes 2½ dozen

FILLING
6 dried Chinese black mushrooms
6 ounces shrimp, shelled and deveined
1 teaspoon salt
1½ tablespoons peanut oil
6 ounces ground pork butt
¼ cup finely diced bamboo shoots
¼ cup finely diced water chestnuts,
*   preferably fresh*
3 green onions, chopped
2 teaspoons sugar
¼ teaspoon white pepper
1 tablespoon Shao Hsing wine or dry sherry
1½ teaspoons light soy sauce
2 teaspoons cornstarch
2 tablespoons chicken stock
2 tablespoons coarsely chopped fresh
*   coriander leaves*
✿
1 recipe Wheat Starch Wrapper Dough (page 89)
Vegetable oil
Light soy sauce, for dipping
Chinese mustard, for dipping

1. Cover the mushrooms with warm water for 20 minutes or until soft and pliable. Remove and squeeze out the excess water. Cut off the stems at the base and discard them. Finely mince the caps.

2. Toss the shrimp with the salt and let them stand 10 minutes. Rinse well with cold water, pat dry thoroughly, and coarsely mince.

3. Preheat a wok or skillet. When hot, add the peanut oil. Add the mushrooms, shrimp, pork butt, bamboo shoots, water chestnuts, and half the green onions; stir-fry over medium-high heat until the pork turns white. Season with the sugar, white pepper, wine, and soy sauce. Combine the cornstarch and chicken stock in a small bowl and mix until smooth; pour into the wok. Stir-fry 1 minute longer. Remove the mixture to a shallow dish and mix in the remaining green onion and the coriander. Allow the filling to cool, then refrigerate it until needed. You should have almost 2 cups of filling.

4. Prepare the wheat starch wrapper dough. Pinch off 1-inch balls of dough until all the dough is divided. Lightly oil one ball and flatten it into a thin 3½-inch circle. (An oiled side of a Chinese cleaver blade is the traditional flattening tool, but a tortilla press or a rolling pin will work too.) Put 1 large teaspoon of filling in the center of the circle. Fold it in half and pinch the edges to seal the filling inside. Repeat with the remaining dough and filling.

5. Place the dumplings in a lightly oiled bamboo steamer or on a heat-resistant plate that fits in a steamer; leave space all around each dumpling. Steam over boiling water for 3 minutes. Serve hot; dip in light soy sauce and Chinese mustard.

HA GOW
Steamed Shrimp Dumplings (China)

These dumplings are a must for dim sum, the Cantonese tea luncheon. Don't be intimidated by the idea of making your own wrappers; they are not difficult. Professional dim sum chefs use a cleaver to flatten the dough—a quick little press and a twist is all it takes. If the cleaver method doesn't work well for you, simply roll out the dough with a rolling pin. You may want to try a special dim sum rolling pin. (It looks like a wooden dowel, ¾ inch in diameter and 12 inches long.) Once steamed, the dumplings may be refrigerated for a few days and reheated in a steamer. For longer storage, freeze on a baking sheet, and once solidly frozen, transfer to a plastic bag.

Makes 2½ dozen

FILLING
½ pound shrimp
1½ teaspoons salt
1½ teaspoons light soy sauce
1 tablespoon Shao Hsing wine or dry sherry
1 teaspoon sugar
1 teaspoon Asian sesame oil
1½ teaspoons cornstarch
¼ cup finely minced bamboo shoots
2 green onions (white section only), finely minced
1 tablespoon minced fresh coriander
❖
1 recipe Wheat Starch Wrapper Dough (page 89)
Vegetable oil
Soy sauce, for dipping

1.   Shell and devein the shrimp. Toss them with 1 teaspoon of the salt and let them sit for 10 minutes. Rinse with cold water, drain, pat dry, and mince. Combine the shrimp with the remaining salt and filling ingredients in a mixing bowl and refrigerate for 2 hours.

2.   Prepare the wheat starch wrapper dough and cut it in half. Roll each half into a long, 1-inch-diameter sausage. Cut each roll into 15 pieces. Dampen a paper towel with oil and lightly wipe the left side of a cleaver blade and a spot close to you on a flat work surface. Take one piece of dough and roll it into a ball. Set it on the work surface and flatten it with the palm of your hand. Then with the oiled side of the cleaver press the dough into a 3½-inch circle. (Use a rolling pin if you prefer.)

3.   With a pastry scraper, carefully lift the wrapper and lay it in the palm of one hand. Put 1 rounded teaspoon of filling off center and fold the wrapper in half to enclose the filling. Make about 8 pleats along one top edge to form

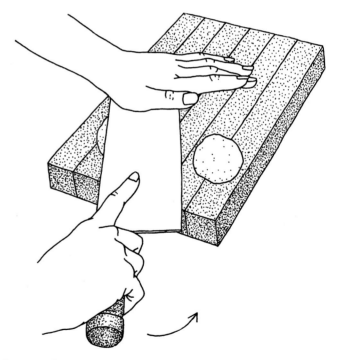

Shaping dough circles

a pouch for the filling (see illustration). Press and seal the pleats against the unpleated side. Repeat with the remaining dough and filling.

4. Lightly oil the bottom of a bamboo steamer basket or a heat-resistant plate that will fit comfortably in a steamer. Arrange the dumplings in the basket or on the plate (they may need to be steamed in batches), leaving a little space between them. Cover and steam over medium-high heat for 8 minutes. Remove the basket and allow the dumplings to cool for 5 minutes before removing them or they will tear. Serve hot or at room temperature, with soy sauce for dipping.

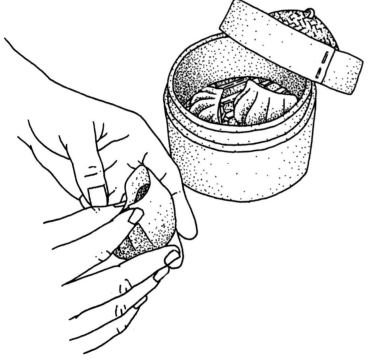

Pleating the dumpling

WHEAT STARCH WRAPPER DOUGH

Wheat starch is flour from which the protein has been removed to make gluten. It is used to make wrappers for several dim sum dumplings. When the wrappers are steamed, they develop a translucent quality which allows the color of the filling to peek through. They are fun and exotic—definitely a conversation piece.

Makes enough for 2½ dozen Ha Gow or Fun Gwau dumplings

> *1 cup wheat starch*
> *¼ cup tapioca starch*
> *1 cup boiling water*
> *1 tablespoon peanut oil*

Combine the wheat starch and tapioca starch in a mixing bowl. When the water reaches a boil, immediately pour it into the starches and stir vigorously with a wooden spoon until the mixture forms a ball. The boiling water cooks the starches. Add the oil and mix together as well as possible. The dough will be quite thick and lumpy. While it is still hot, gather it up and knead it on a lightly oiled surface until smooth and well blended, about 3 minutes. It should feel a bit rubbery and putty-like. Cover it with a damp towel; it is ready to make into Ha Gow or Fun Gwau.

WOO GWAU
Taro Root Turnovers
(China)

These turnovers, seldom made at home, are one of the many specialties of Chinese tearooms. The recipe may sound intimidating, but that is only because it has many stages. In fact, none of the steps is difficult, and much of the preparation can be done ahead. I do recommend using a food processor to make the taro dough; personally I wouldn't make the dough by hand.

Makes 20 to 24

TARO DOUGH
2 pounds taro root (see Note)
⅔ cup wheat starch, plus more for dusting
1 cup boiling water
1 teaspoon salt
1 teaspoon sugar
½ cup lard or shortening

FILLING
6 Chinese dried black mushrooms
6 ounces shrimp, shelled and deveined
1 teaspoon salt
6 ounces boneless chicken thigh, chopped
3 tablespoons minced bamboo shoots
2 tablespoons chopped green onion
1 teaspoon ginger juice or grated ginger
½ teaspoon sugar
Large pinch white pepper
1½ teaspoons cornstarch
1½ teaspoons dark soy sauce
½ teaspoon Asian sesame oil
1½ teaspoons oyster sauce
1½ teaspoons Shao Hsing wine or dry sherry

✿

2 tablespoons peanut oil, plus more for
*   deep-frying*
Wheat starch, for dusting
Soy sauce, for dipping
Chinese mustard, for dipping

1. *To make taro dough,* peel the taro root and cut it into ½-inch slices. Steam the slices until tender, about 30 minutes. When a chopstick pierces a slice easily, it is done. (Don't be alarmed by the purplish-grey color it turns when cooked; this is normal.) Cool the taro, then process it in a food processor to the consistency of mashed potatoes. Discard any lumps.

2. Put the wheat starch in a bowl. Bring the water to a boil; immediately pour it into the starch and mix it by hand into a smooth, fairly thick, soft dough. Add the dough, salt, sugar, and lard to the taro and knead, or process in a food processor, until thoroughly blended. Refrigerate the dough until firm, 2 hours or longer.

3. *To prepare the filling,* cover the mushrooms with water for 20 minutes or until soft and pliable. Squeeze out the excess water. Cut off and discard the stems; mince the caps. Toss the shrimp with 1 teaspoon salt. Rinse well with cold water, pat dry thoroughly, and coarsely mince. In a bowl combine the mushrooms and shrimp with the remaining filling ingredients.

4. Preheat a wok or skillet. When hot, add the 2 tablespoons of peanut oil. Add the filling mixture and stir-fry over medium-high heat until the chicken turns white, about 5 minutes. Remove the mixture to a shallow dish and allow it to cool. Refrigerate until ready to use.

5. *To make the turnovers,* take a 2-inch ball of taro dough and shape it into a flat, oval disk, slightly more than ¼ inch thick. Press a pocket in the center with a finger and fill it with a rounded tablespoon of filling. Mold the dough around the filling and into a lemon shape; pinch the edges

Left to right: Ha Gow, Four Seasons Dumplings, Fun Gwau, Woo Gwau

together to seal in the filling. Make certain that the dough around the filling is ¼ inch thick or the turnover will burst when frying. Dust the turnover with wheat starch and set it aside. Repeat with the remaining dough and filling.

6.   Preheat the oven to 200°. Preheat a wok and add oil to a depth of 2 inches; heat the oil to 360°. Gently slide 4 or 5 turnovers into the oil and fry until golden brown, about 3 minutes. Remove with a strainer and drain on a wire rack or paper towels. Keep hot in the oven while cooking the remaining turnovers. Serve hot; dip into soy sauce and Chinese mustard.

NOTE Taro root, the potato of Asian cooking, is a starchy tuber with a brown hairy covering. There are many varieties. Try to find large ones with purple veins in the flesh; they have the best flavor and aroma. (Some Asian produce stores will leave a cut one out to let you see the creamy white flesh with fine purple veins.) Store taro as you would a potato, although it will keep for only about a week. Peel with a knife or vegetable peeler before using.

FOUR SEASONS DUMPLINGS
(*China*)

These dumplings, filled with a minced pork and shrimp filling, are accompanied by four garnishes, chosen to represent the seasons of the year. Green peas symbolize spring; red bell pepper, summer; orange carrot, fall; and brown mushrooms, winter.

Makes 2½ to 3 dozen

FILLING
6 ounces shrimp, shelled and deveined
1 teaspoon salt
12 ounces finely minced pork butt
1 green onion, finely minced
1 teaspoon ginger, grated or finely minced
¼ cup bamboo shoots, finely diced
1 teaspoon sugar
Pinch of white pepper
1 tablespoon light soy sauce
1 tablespoon Shao Hsing wine or dry sherry
1 teaspoon Asian sesame oil
1 tablespoon cornstarch
❀
1 package sui mai *wrappers or thin* won ton *skins*

GARNISHES
3 dried Chinese black mushrooms, soaked
    in water for 20 minutes, squeezed dry,
    and cut into pea-size pieces
1 carrot, cut into pea-size pieces
40 ¼-inch squares red bell pepper or diced ham
80 fresh shelled peas or ¼ cup blanched
    spinach leaves, chopped
❀
Vegetable oil
Soy sauce, for dipping
Chinese mustard, for dipping

1.   Toss the shrimp with the salt and let them stand for 10 minutes. Rinse thoroughly with cold water, pat dry, and cut into ¼-inch dice. Place the shrimp in a mixing bowl and add the remaining filling ingredients; mix well. If you are not going to fill the dumplings right away, refrigerate the filling.

2.   Place a heaping teaspoon of filling in the center of a siu mai wrapper. Fold the wrapper in half over the filling. Moisten a point in the center of each semi-circular edge with water and pinch them together. Bring the two outer corners to the center and pinch them together, making an X where the edges meet and creating 4 small pouches. Carefully fill each of the pouches with a different garnish. Repeat with the remaining wrappers, filling, and garnishes.

3.   Lightly oil the bottom of a steaming basket. Arrange the dumplings in the basket leaving space between them. If you prefer, you may use an oiled, heat-resistant plate that will fit comfortably into a steamer. Cover and steam over boiling water for 10 to 12 minutes. Serve hot, with soy sauce and hot Chinese mustard for dipping.

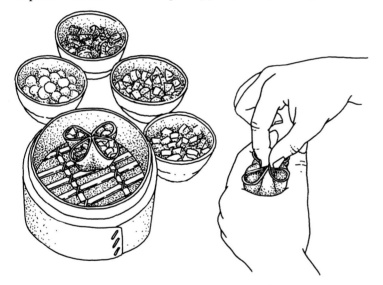

Pinching the wrapper to create four pouches

EASY CHEESE AND SHRIMP GYOZAS
(East/West)

Cheese and cream are not traditional ingredients in Asian cooking. However, I enjoy the subtle flavor of a mild cheese, such as Monterey Jack, and the way it works in this *gyoza* (Japanese-style potsticker) recipe. The cheese acts as a velvety binder that melts in your mouth; the cream is used to make a lime-scented sauce.

A dozen gyozas makes a nice appetizer serving for four, but it's not really practical to make just a dozen at a time. This recipe makes 4 dozen, and the rest can be frozen for another use. The sauce recipe is enough for a dozen; if you want to make more, simply multiply the sauce ingredients, but bear in mind that you will have to make the sauce separately as part of each batch. Freeze extra uncooked gyozas on a baking sheet; when frozen, transfer them to a freezer bag. Do not defrost before browning.

Makes 48 (16 servings)

*½ pound medium shrimp (41 to 50 per pound),
    shelled and deveined*
1½ teaspoons salt
1 teaspoon finely minced ginger or ginger juice
2 teaspoons Shao Hsing wine or dry sherry
1 teaspoon cornstarch
5 water chestnuts (fresh), finely chopped
2 green onions, chopped
1½ tablespoons chopped fresh coriander
2 Chinese sausages, finely chopped
*1¼ cups grated Monterey Jack cheese
    (about 5 ounces)*
1 package (12 to 16 ounces) round siu mai
    wrappers or won ton wrappers

LIME CREAM SAUCE *(serves 4)*
1 tablespoon oil
⅔ cup chicken stock
½ cup whipping cream
1 tablespoon lime juice
Salt and white pepper, to taste
Fresh coriander

1. Toss the shrimp with 1 teaspoon of the salt and let them stand for 10 minutes. Rinse thoroughly, drain, and pat dry. Finely chop the shrimp and put them into a mixing bowl. Add the remaining salt and the ginger, wine, cornstarch, water chestnuts, green onions, coriander, sausages, and cheese; mix thoroughly.

2. If you are using won ton wrappers, trim the corners to make them round. Place 1 heaping teaspoon of the filling in the center of a wrapper. Moisten the edge of the wrapper with water and fold it in half to enclose the filling and form a half circle. Pinch the edges together to seal. Set the gyoza on a baking sheet; cover it with a towel. Repeat with the remaining filling and wrappers.

3. To cook and sauce 4 servings, add 1 tablespoon of oil to a 10-inch nonstick skillet and set it over medium heat. Arrange 12 gyozas in a single layer in the pan; pan-fry for 1 minute or until lightly browned. Turn the gyozas over and brown the other side, about 1 minute longer. Add the chicken stock; shake the pan to prevent the gyozas from sticking. Cover and cook at a low boil for 2 minutes. Remove the gyozas to a plate and keep them warm.

4. Increase the heat to high and add the cream; bring it to a boil and cook, stirring, until thickened, about 45 seconds. Stir in the lime juice; season to taste with salt and pepper.

5. To serve, divide the sauce among 4 plates; arrange 3 gyozas on each. Garnish with fresh coriander.

NASI GORENG
Festive Fried Rice
(Indonesia)

Asians serve fried rice for breakfast, lunch, or as a snack. A home-style dish, fried rice is an efficient way of using up leftover rice. It can be anything from a simple bowl of leftover steamed rice fried in oil and salt to an elaborate one-dish meal complete with assorted meat, fish, poultry, and vegetables. Although it is not customary, fried rice makes a delicious light dinner.

Nasi Goreng, Indonesian-style fried rice, makes a tasty first course for an informal dinner. It is cooked with typical Indonesian seasonings—shallots, garlic, turmeric, chiles, shrimp paste, tamarind, and a generous sprinkling of *ketjap manis,* the thick, syrupy, sweet and savory soy sauce of Indonesia. In this recipe, as in all fried rice recipes, every ingredient is optional and may be omitted except, of course, the rice.

Serves 8

1-inch chunk tamarind pulp
½ cup boiling water
½ cup chopped shallots (about 4 shallots)
1½ tablespoons chopped garlic (about 3 cloves)
2 red serrano chiles, chopped, or *1 teaspoon Indonesian ground chili paste* (sambal ulek)
1 teaspoon shrimp paste or anchovy paste (optional)
½ teaspoon turmeric
1 teaspoon salt, or to taste
3 tablespoons vegetable oil (more if needed)
6 ounces medium shrimp (41 to 50 per pound), shelled and deveined
½ cup diced red bell pepper
½ cup green peas
1 cup shredded purple cabbage

6 cups cooked long-grain white rice (cold)
2 tablespoons ketjap manis or dark soy sauce
1 tablespoon light soy sauce
3 green onions, thinly sliced
½ cup diced cooked chicken
½ cup diced Chinese barbecued pork or ham

GARNISHES
Fresh coriander leaves
2 large eggs for omelet shreds (optional, see page 26)
3 tablespoons Crisp Fried Shallot Flakes (page 26)
½ English cucumber, thinly sliced

1.   Cover the tamarind pulp with the boiling water. Mash the fibers and seeds with the back of a fork. When the tamarind is dissolved, strain it; reserve ⅓ cup of the tamarind water.

2.   Chop the shallots, garlic, chiles, shrimp paste, turmeric, and salt into as smooth a paste as possible in a mini-food processor, or pound them smooth in a mortar.

3.   Preheat a wok or skillet over medium-high heat. When hot, add the oil and the spice paste; cook gently until brown. Turn the heat to high and add the shrimp. Stir-fry until they turn bright orange, about 30 seconds. Add the bell pepper, peas, and cabbage; stir-fry until the vegetables are cooked but still crisp, about 1½ minutes. If needed, add a little more oil; add the rice and stir-fry, breaking up the lumps of rice. When each rice grain is separate, add the tamarind water, kepjap manis, light soy sauce, green onions, chicken, and barbecued pork; mix together evenly. Check for seasoning and adjust if necessary with soy sauce and/or ketjap manis.

4.   Transfer the fried rice to a serving plate. Garnish with coriander leaves, the shredded omelet, and fried shallots. Arrange the cucumbers around the edge.

CANTONESE ROAST DUCK CONGEE
(China)

Congee, also called *jook*, is a rice soup served throughout China and Southeast Asia. The style of preparation varies from region to region. It may be anything from a simple rice soup made with water to a rich jook based on duck or turkey stock (turkey jook after Thanksgiving is becoming a tradition for Chinese-Americans). It is served with a variety of toppings or side dishes. My favorite is Chinese crullers or "Chinese doughnuts," a deep-fried savory pastry which looks like a fried baguette. It is dipped into the soup to soak it up.

Serves 6

1 roast duck carcass (see Note)
Juices from 1 roast duck
2 1-inch chunks ginger
3 whole green onions
3 quarts water
⅔ cup rice, washed until the water runs clear
Salt to taste

CONDIMENTS AND ACCOMPANIMENTS
White pepper
Soy sauce
Sesame oil
Chopped green onions
Fresh coriander leaves
Chinese crullers, sliced diagonally

1. Chop the duck carcass into large pieces. Place the pieces in a large stockpot with the juices from the duck's cavity and the ginger, onions, and water. Bring to a boil, skim the surface, and cover. Simmer for 2 hours. Strain the resulting stock, skim off the excess fat, and measure out 8 cups. Reserve the remainder for other uses.

2. Pour the 8 cups of stock into a deep saucepan. Add the rice and bring to a boil. Stir to loosen the rice grains from the bottom of the pan. Reduce the heat to low and cover the pan. Simmer until the rice thickens to a porridge consistency, about 1½ to 2 hours. Thin the congee with water or chicken stock if it is too thick. Serve hot with the condiments and accompaniments alongside.

NOTE You need only the carcass and juices from a roast duck for this recipe. Buy a whole roast duck at a Cantonese delicatessen or restaurant. (Ask for the juices from the cavity as well.) Remove the meat and use it for stir-frying or a salad. Chop the carcass into pieces.

KHAO PAD SUPPAROT
Rice Fried with Pineapple
(Thailand)

To make this into a very pretty party dish, start with a whole pineapple. Cut off the top and carefully cut out the pineapple meat; coarsely chop 1 cup for the fried rice. When it is done cooking, spoon the rice into the pineapple shell and serve from it.

Serves 4 to 6

> *3 to 4 tablespoons vegetable oil*
> *2 shallots, chopped*
> *3 cloves garlic, chopped*
> *2 fresh red chiles, sliced*
> *¼ pound pork butt, coarsely chopped*
> *6 ounces medium shrimp (41 to 50 per pound),*
>   *shelled and deveined*
> *4 cups cold cooked rice*
> *3 green onions, chopped*
> *1 teaspoon dried shrimp powder with chile*
>   *(optional)*
> *1 teaspoon sugar*
> *2 tablespoons Thai fish sauce* (nam pla)
> *1 tablespoon soy sauce*
> *2 eggs*
> *Salt, to taste*
> *1 cup fresh pineapple, cut into ¼-inch chunks*
> *4 ounces cooked crabmeat*
> *2 tablespoons Crisp Fried Shallot Flakes (page 26)*
> *Fresh sprigs of mint or coriander, for garnish*

1.   Preheat a wok over medium-high heat. When hot, add the oil, shallots, garlic, and chiles; cook until lightly browned. Increase the heat to high, add the pork, and stir-fry until browned. Add the shrimp; toss until they turn bright orange. Gently break up the lumps of cold rice and add it to the wok. Toss in the green onions, shrimp powder, sugar, fish sauce, and soy sauce. Continue tossing and stirring over high heat until evenly mixed.

2.   Push the rice up the side of the wok. Break the eggs into the center, season with salt, and scramble the eggs with your spatula, keeping them in the center. Allow them to cook until set, then toss them together with the rice. Fold in the pineapple and crabmeat to mix and heat through. Serve garnished with Crisp Fried Shallot Flakes and mint or coriander sprigs.

PORK "SPAGHETTI SAUCE" FOR RICE
(*Vietnam*)

The first time I had Vietnamese spaghetti sauce, I was pleasantly surprised—it was served over rice. It brought back memories of my Cantonese culinary upbringing. Whether the menu was Chinese or Western, my mother always served rice, even with spaghetti, fettuccine, potatoes, or any other starch. This "spaghetti sauce" tastes best served over rice.

Serves 6

1 tablespoon vegetable oil
1½ pounds ground pork
1½ tablespoons sugar
1½ tablespoons lime juice
2 serrano chiles, seeded and chopped
4½ tablespoons Vietnamese fish sauce
    (nuoc mam)
¼ cup chopped garlic
1½ cups chopped shallots or onions
½ teaspoon ground black pepper
5 large tomatoes, seeded and chopped
¼ cup tomato paste
1½ cups chicken stock
6 cups (approximately) hot steamed rice
Nuoc Cham Dipping Sauce (see Note, page 69)
Fresh coriander leaves, for garnish

1.   Heat the oil in a saucepan over high heat. Add the pork and saute until lightly browned, about 5 minutes. Break up any lumps. Add the sugar, lime juice, chiles, and 1½ tablespoons of the fish sauce. Cook a minute longer. Remove and set aside in a bowl.

2.   Return the saucepan to medium heat; add the garlic, shallots, and black pepper. Fry until the garlic and shallots are wilted and fragrant. Add the tomatoes and cook until the mixture is reduced to a slightly lumpy sauce, about 5 minutes. Return the pork to the pan, add the tomato paste, remaining fish sauce, and the chicken stock; simmer for 10 minutes. Serve hot over steamed rice. Add a few drops of Nuoc Cham Dipping Sauce and garnish with coriander leaves.

SAVORY CHICKEN AND RICE IN A LOTUS LEAF
(China)

Foods wrapped in dried lotus leaves become infused with an exotic earthy flavor. If lotus leaves are not available, you can wrap the rice filling in oiled parchment. Besides being an unusual appetizer, this dish can be served as a snack, for lunch, or as a light meal. Note that the first step must be done the night before. Because lotus leaves vary so much in size, eight packets may require anywhere from four to ten leaves. (Larger leaves can be split in half, smaller leaves may need to be overlapped.)

Makes 8 packets

> 8 *large dried lotus leaves*
> 1 *cup long-grain rice*
> ¾ *cup sweet glutinous rice (see Note)*
> 2 *cups chicken stock*
> 3 *Chinese sausages* (lop cheong), *cut diagonally into 1-inch slices*
> 8 *Chinese dried black mushrooms, soaked in warm water until soft and pliable (about 30 minutes)*
> 2 *tablespoons small dried shrimp, soaked in warm water for 30 minutes*
> 1 *whole chicken breast, boned and skinned*
> 2 *tablespoons soy sauce, plus more for dipping*
> 1 *teaspoon sugar*
> ¼ *teaspoon white pepper*
> 1 *teaspoon Asian sesame oil*

CHICKEN MARINADE
> ½ *teaspoon grated ginger*
> 2 *teaspoons soy sauce*
> 2 *teaspoons dry vermouth or Shao Hsing wine*
> ½ *teaspoon sugar*

> ¼ *teaspoon white pepper*
> 1 *teaspoon Asian sesame oil*

1. The night before, pour boiling water over the lotus leaves and let them soak for 1 hour. Rinse and squeeze them dry. Mix the long-grain and glutinous rice together in a large bowl. Wash the rice under running cold water; gently stir and rub the grains between your fingers to loosen all the excess starch. Continue until the water runs clear. Drain thoroughly. Mix the rice with the chicken stock in a 2-quart saucepan; soak overnight in the refrigerator.

2. The next day, set the saucepan of rice uncovered over high heat; bring to a boil. Stir just enough to loosen the rice grains. Reduce the heat to medium-high and boil until the liquid is absorbed, about 8 to 10 minutes. Put the sausages on top of the rice and cover the pan. Reduce the heat to low and cook for 20 minutes. Turn off the heat but do not remove the cover. Let the rice stand for 10 minutes, then, with a wet wooden spoon, transfer it to a large bowl; set aside.

3. Squeeze the mushrooms dry. Cut off the stems at the base and discard them; cut the caps in half. Combine the marinade ingredients in a medium bowl. Cut the chicken breast into ¾-inch chunks and toss it with the marinade. Add the mushrooms and marinate for 20 minutes. Drain and coarsely chop the shrimp.

4. In a small bowl combine the soy sauce, sugar, white pepper, and sesame oil; mix into the cooked rice. Add the chicken-mushroom mixture and the shrimp.

5. Fold a lotus leaf in half and put it on a cutting board. If the middle stem or edges are tough and hard, trim and discard them. (If the leaves are small, you may need to overlap halves.) Divide the rice mixture into 8 portions; place one portion in the center of a leaf half. Fold the edges over

the rice to make a 4-inch square packet. Tie it with twine. Repeat with the remaining leaves and rice. Arrange the packets in a single layer in a bamboo steaming basket.

6.   Prepare a wok for steaming (see page 13). Steam the packets over medium-high heat for 20 minutes. Remove them from the steamer and cut each packet across the top to expose its contents. Serve with small dishes of soy sauce for dipping.

NOTE Sweet glutinous rice is also known as "sticky rice" because when it is cooked it becomes sticky. It is used to make poultry stuffing and leaf-wrapped rice packages; it is called sweet rice because it is often used to make sweet dishes. Soak it overnight before cooking for the best results.

LITTLE DISHES FOR BUFFETS

Crab Claws "Stuffed" with
    Shrimp Mousse
Cantonese Barbecued Pork (Cha Siu)
Fish Mousse Grilled in a
    Banana Leaf
Meatballs Wrapped in Pasta
Shrimp and Sugar Cane Rolls
Chicken Wing Adobo
Meatballs in Spicy Peanut Sauce
Roast Duck and Melon Salad
Spicy Sesame Jellyfish Salad
Five-Spice Grilled Quail
Lady Fingers Sambal
Pan-Fried Radish Cakes
Son-in-Law Eggs
Miso Barbecued Short Ribs
Shrimp and Potato Toasts

Meatballs Wrapped in Pasta
(recipe, pg. 112)

CRAB CLAWS "STUFFED" WITH SHRIMP MOUSSE
(China)

This is an appetizer that will really grab you. It can be made with any medium-sized crab claws, including West Coast Dungeness crab or larger East Coast blue crab. Order the cooked crab claws in advance from your fish market. Or look for plastic bags of claws in the freezer sections of better Asian markets.

Serves 8

> 1 pound medium shrimp, shelled and deveined
> 1 teaspoon salt
> 8 water chestnuts, preferably fresh, peeled
> 1 large green onion (white part only)
> 1 tablespoon Shao Hsing wine or dry sherry
> 1 teaspoon grated ginger
> ¼ teaspoon sugar
> 2 tablespoons cornstarch
> 3 tablespoons chicken stock
> 1 large egg white, beaten until fluffy but not stiff
> ½ cup flour
> ½ cup fine panko or bread crumbs
> 2 large eggs, beaten with ¼ teaspoon salt
> 16 cooked crab claws
> Peanut or corn oil for deep-frying

1. Toss the shrimp with the salt and let them sit for 10 minutes. Rinse with cold water, drain thoroughly, and blot dry.

2. Finely mince the water chestnuts and green onion in a food processor. Add the shrimp and process to a smooth paste (about 15 seconds). Add the wine, ginger, sugar, and cornstarch and mix with a pulsing action several times until thoroughly blended. With the motor running, pour the chicken stock in through the feed tube and process until the mixture is light and fluffy, about 5 seconds. Add the egg white and mix with a pulsing action until blended. Cover and refrigerate for 1 hour.

3. Spread the flour and panko on separate plates, with the beaten eggs in a shallow bowl in between.

4. Crack the crab claws carefully and remove the shell from all but the pincers, exposing most of the meat. Divide the shrimp mixture into 16 equal portions. Wet your hands with oil or water and carefully mold 1 portion of shrimp mixture around the base of each claw, forming a ball about 1½ inches in diameter with most of the pincers exposed. Holding the claw by the pincers, lightly dust the shrimp mousse with flour, then dip it into beaten egg to coat it thoroughly, then roll it in the breadcrumbs. Pat the crumbs in place with a dry hand. Lay the battered claws on waxed paper and refrigerate for 15 minutes or longer to let the coatings set.

5. Preheat a wok over medium-high heat. Add oil to a depth of 2 inches and heat to 360°. Holding onto the pincers, gently slide about 4 crab claws into the hot oil (or as many as will fit without crowding or reducing the temperature of the oil). Fry until golden brown, about 5 minutes. Remove with a slotted spoon and drain on paper towels. Continue with the remaining crab claws. Serve hot. Although they taste best right from the fryer, they can be made in advance and reheated in a 350° oven.

CHA SIU
Cantonese Barbecued Pork
(China)

Think of these sweet, glazed strips of roast pork as the ham of Asia. Both Chinese and Southeast Asian cooks serve *cha siu* as a main dish, or as a meat addition or a tasty garnish in many stir-fry mixtures, soups, noodle dishes, and fried rice.

Most Chinese cooks purchase their *cha siu* already prepared at a "roasting shop" (delicatessen); however, it is very easy to make at home, and the results are not as garishly red as some commercial versions made with food coloring. Pork butt is preferred for its fat, but other shoulder cuts as well as tenderloin are also good choices. You can never make too much, as it freezes well. Half of this recipe will serve eight as a buffet dish; reserve the remainder for other uses. (See Baked Barbecued Pork Buns, page 46.)

Makes about 2½ pounds

> *3 to 3½ pounds pork tenderloin, shoulder, or butt*
> *4 tablespoons dark soy sauce*
> *2 tablespoons light soy sauce*
> *3 tablespoons sugar*
> *3 tablespoons honey*
> *4 tablespoons hoisin sauce*
> *1 tablespoon grated fresh ginger*
> *2 tablespoons Shao Hsing wine or dry sherry*
> *1½ teaspoons salt*

ACCOMPANIMENTS
Chinese Hot Mustard (see page 19)
Toasted sesame seeds (see page 27)

1.   Remove and discard the excess fat from the pork. Cut the pork lengthwise (with the grain) into 2-inch-wide strips 5 to 6 inches long. Put them into a large bowl.

2.   Combine the soy sauces, sugar, honey, hoisin sauce, ginger, wine, and salt. Pour the mixture over the meat and rub it in well. Cover and marinate in the refrigerator at least overnight and up to 3 days. Turn the meat several times.

3.   Preheat the oven to 350°. Place the pork strips on a broiler pan lined with foil. Roast for 30 minutes, turning once halfway through. Increase the heat to 425° and roast 10 minutes longer. Remove from the oven and let cool before slicing.

4.   To serve as a buffet dish, cut across the grain into ¼-inch-thick slices. Arrange on a platter with saucers of Hot Mustard Dipping Sauce and toasted sesame seeds. Use toothpicks to dip a slice of pork into the mustard then into the sesame seeds.

VARIATION Cantonese Barbecued Pork Spareribs are delicious when marinated and cooked in the same way. Have the butcher cut a slab of ribs crosswise into 4-inch-wide sections. Remove and discard the excess fat and lightly score both sides with crisscross cuts 2 inches apart. Marinate as directed above, preferably for 2 days. Roast as directed above. When the meat begins to pull away from the bones the ribs are done. Cut into individual ribs to serve.

Fish Mousse Grilled in a Banana Leaf

OTAK OTAK
Fish Mouse Grilled in a Banana Leaf (Singapore)

These banana leaf packets filled with a spicy fish mousse make great grill-it-yourself barbecued appetizers. The banana jackets make them wonderfully easy to hold in your hand as picnic food. Or, if you prefer, the filling may be spread on toast points for a more formal presentation.

Otak Otak comes in many variations throughout Southeast Asia. Each version contains a *rempah,* the Malay name for the hand-pounded seasoning pastes which are the *bouquet garni* of Southeast Asian cooking. The traditional Singapore Nonya rempah includes chiles, garlic, shallots, lemongrass, turmeric, candlenuts, and shrimp paste, although other spices and herbs may be used to enhance a particular dish. Like curry pastes, rempahs are traditionally pounded in a mortar. Although a hand-pounded paste is better, it is time-consuming and laborious for the average American cook. I recommend starting the paste in a spice mill and/or a mini-food processor, switching to a mortar for a final pounding to smooth out the rough edges.

In Singapore, Otak Otak is usually made with a Spanish mackerel called *tenggiri,* but this recipe was developed with milder white-fleshed fish.

Makes 24

> *Rempah (see below)*
> *1½ pounds white fish fillets*
> *2 teaspoons salt*
> *1 tablespoon sugar*
> *½ teaspoon white pepper*
> *1 large egg, lightly beaten*

> *4 fresh or frozen Kaffir lime leaves (daun limau perut), if available; or substitute fresh citrus leaves*
> *24 6-inch squares of fresh or frozen banana leaf or aluminum foil*
> *24 medium shrimp (about ½ pound), peeled and deveined*

1. Prepare the Rempah on page 111.

2. Pat the fish dry and cut it into 2-inch pieces. Put the fish in the workbowl of a food processor and chop into a fine paste. Add the salt, sugar, white pepper, and egg and process until fully incorporated, about 5 seconds. Transfer the mixture to a large bowl and stir in the cooled rempah. Beat with a wooden spoon or mix with your hands until smooth, about 5 minutes. Remove the spines from the lime leaves and cut the leaves into very fine shreds. Fold them into the fish mixture.

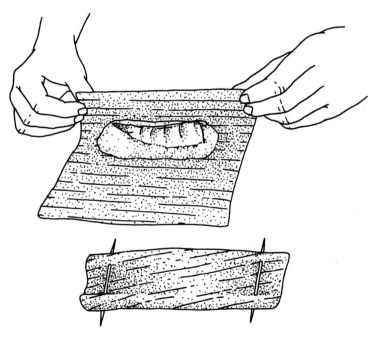

Folding the banana leaf packets

3. For each packet, dip a square of banana leaf into boiling water for 1 to 2 minutes; pat dry. Spread 2 to 3 tablespoons of the fish mixture down the middle of the leaf to within 1 inch of the ends (see illustration). Place a shrimp in the middle of the fish mousse and pat it into the filling to lie flat. Fold the long edges over the filling (they should overlap in the center) to make a flat long packet. Press down lightly to flatten the packet a bit; press the ends shut and seal with toothpicks. (Packets may be prepared to this point up to 2 hours ahead of time and refrigerated.)

4. Place the banana leaf packets on a grill 3 to 4 inches over a medium-hot fire and cook for 3 minutes per side (open one to test for doneness before serving). Serve hot, warm, or at room temperature.

VARIATION Otak Otak can also be steamed. Put the fish packets on a steaming tray in a wok filled with boiling water and steam over medium-high heat for 5 minutes.

REMPAH
Spice Paste

8 dried red chiles
2 stalks fresh lemongrass or 1 tablespoon
    lemongrass powder or zest of ½ lemon
2 quarter-size slices fresh galangal
    or 1 quarter-size slice dried galangal,
    soaked in warm water for 30 minutes
6 candlenuts (buah kera) or macadamia nuts
2 shallots
4 cloves garlic
½ teaspoon turmeric
¾ teaspoon ground coriander seeds
½ teaspoon shrimp paste or anchovy paste
1 cup thick coconut milk

1. Cut the chiles just below the stem. Shake the chiles to loosen the seeds. Discard the stem and seeds. Put the chiles into a bowl and cover them with warm water; soak 15 minutes (1 hour is better, if you have the time).

2. Cut off and discard the root from the lemongrass. Remove the tough outer leaves until you see a light purple ring. Use only the tender white mid-section; chop coarsely.

3. With the motor running, drop the lemongrass down the feed tube of a mini-processor; chop as fine as possible. Add the galangal; chop as fine as possible. Add the chiles and chop as fine as possible. Add the candlenuts, shallots, garlic, turmeric, ground coriander, and shrimp paste and process together into a paste (this may take 2 to 3 minutes); scrape down the sides of the work bowl as necessary.

4. Heat ¼ cup thick coconut milk in a saucepan over medium-high heat; stir continuously until thick and oily. Add the contents of the processor and cook gently until the mixture is fragrant and oily, about 5 minutes. Add the remaining coconut milk and bring to a boil, stirring constantly; cook until incorporated. Let cool before adding to the fish mixture. The rempah can be made a few hours ahead of time.

MOO SARONG
Meatballs Wrapped in Pasta (Thailand)

These delicious deep-fried appetizers look like crispy golden balls of rolled yarn. The center is a meatball stuffed with a morsel of salted duck egg yolk, a favorite food of Asians. The salted duck egg and the Sriracha sauce, a commercially prepared chili sauce, are available in Asian grocery stores.

Makes about 24

½ pound thin fresh Chinese egg noodles
1 teaspoon black peppercorns
1 tablespoon fresh coriander roots
4 cloves garlic
1 teaspoon salt
1 pound finely minced or ground pork butt
1 egg
1 tablespoon flour
½ cup finely minced water chestnuts or
*   bamboo shoots*
4 salted duck eggs (optional)
Peanut oil for deep-frying
Thai Sweet and Sour Cucumber Relish (page 27)
Sriracha sauce, for dipping

1.   Bring a pot of water to a boil. Add the noodles and stir for 10 seconds. (The water probably won't come back to a full boil, but the noodles do not have to be fully cooked at this point because they will be fried later.) Pour them into a colander and drain. Rinse with cold water. Set aside.

2.   Pound or grind the pepper to a powder in a mortar, spice mill, or mini-chopper. Add the coriander root, garlic, and salt and work into a paste. Combine with the pork, egg, flour, and water chestnuts in a medium bowl and mix thoroughly. Cover and refrigerate until firm, at least 1 hour.

3.   Crack the duck eggs. The whites will be gelatinous, but the yolks should be solid, even more so than a hard-cooked egg. Discard the whites and cut the yolks into ¼-inch pieces. Form the meat mixture into balls about 1½ inches in diameter (no larger or they will not cook through). Bury a piece of duck egg yolk in the middle of each meatball. Starting with two or three strands of noodle, embed the ends into the meatball and wind the noodles around the ball as if winding a ball of yarn, until the ball is completely covered. Wrap the remaining balls in the same manner.

4.   Preheat a wok and add oil to a depth of 2 inches. Heat the oil to 375°. Fry the meatballs a few at a time until golden brown, 4 to 5 minutes. Drain well on paper towels and serve warm or at room temperature with Thai Sweet and Sour Cucumber Relish or Sriracha sauce for dipping.

Shrimp and Sugar Cane Rolls

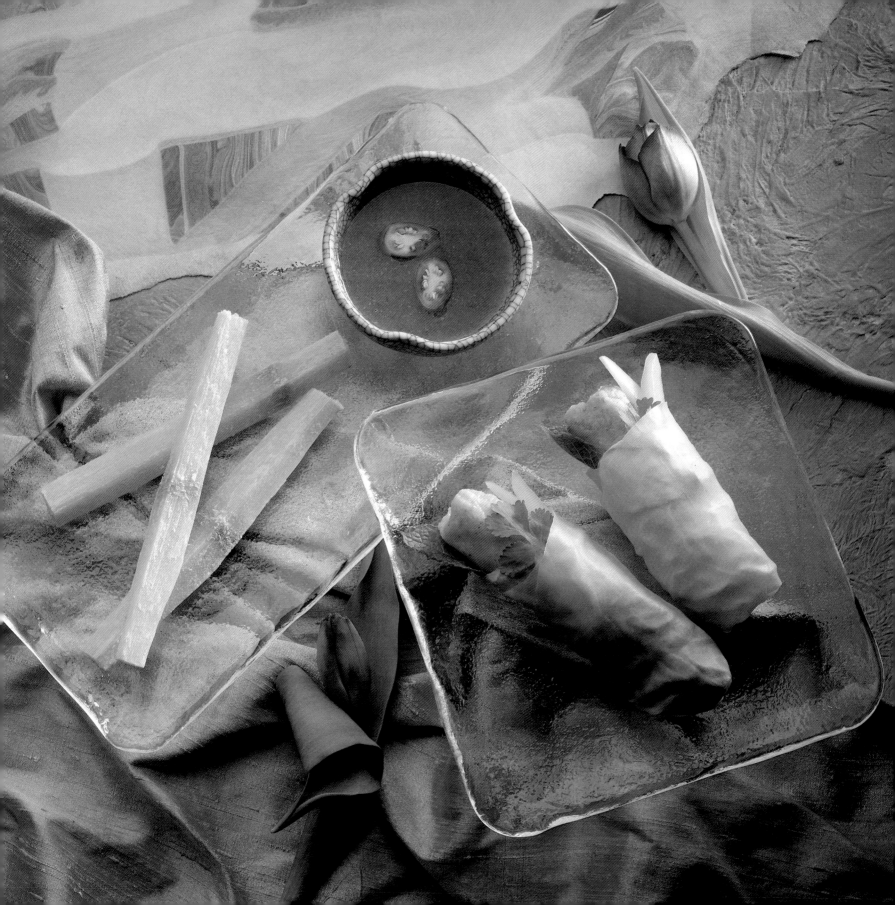

CHAO TOM
Shrimp and Sugar Cane Rolls
(Vietnam)

Molding a ground shrimp mixture around a piece of sugar cane gives an exotic appearance to this traditional Vietnamese dish. It also enhances the flavor; the sweetness of the sugar cane subtly melts into the shrimp paste, and chewing it complements the taste of both the shrimp and the accompanying vegetables.

In the traditional Vietnamese home, the shrimp rolls are grilled over a small charcoal-fired earthen stove set on the table. (The same stove is also used for simmering and boiling as well as grilling.) I have broiled this dish in the oven, with excellent results. Try it as a buffet appetizer or as a first course for a dinner party.

Serves 6

   1 pound shrimp, shelled and deveined
   2 teaspoons salt
   2 cloves garlic
   2 shallots
   2 teaspoons sugar
   ¼ teaspoon black pepper
   1 tablespoon toasted rice powder (see page 23)
   1 tablespoon Vietnamese fish sauce (nuoc mam)
   2 tablespoons ice water
   ¼ cup vegetable oil
   3 6-inch-long canned sugar cane sections,
      about 1 inch in diameter
   1 cucumber, peeled and cut into thin slivers
   1 cup fresh mint leaves
   1 cup fresh coriander leaves
   12 butter or red leaf lettuce leaves
   12 8-inch round rice papers
   Nuoc Cham Dipping Sauce (see Note, page 69)

1.   Toss the shrimp with salt and let them sit for 10 minutes. Rinse with cold water, drain thoroughly, and blot dry.

2.   Mince the garlic and shallots finely in a food processor. Add the sugar, pepper, toasted rice powder, fish sauce, and shrimp and process into a smooth paste. With the machine running, pour the ice water through the feed tube; continue processing until the shrimp is light and fluffy, about 10 seconds. Cover and refrigerate until thoroughly chilled.

3.   Pour the oil into a small bowl. Oil a wire cooling rack and place it on a baking sheet. Cut the sugar cane pieces lengthwise into quarters to make 12 long strips. Dip your fingers into the oil, then take about 2 tablespoons shrimp paste and evenly mold it into a 1-inch cylinder around a sugar cane strip, leaving 1 inch free at each end. Arrange the rolls on the rack diagonally, and keep them from touching each other.

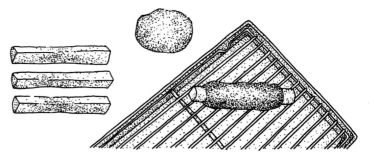

About 2 tablespoons of shrimp paste is molded around each sugar cane strip.

4.   Arrange the cucumber, mint and coriander leaves, and lettuce on a platter; set aside. Broil the shrimp rolls about 6 inches from the heat, turning once, until the edges are bright orange and the filling feels firm to the touch, 2 to 3 minutes per side.

5.   If serving as stand-up party food, soften the rice papers ahead of time as directed on page 70 and arrange them on a platter, folded in half, with the dipping sauce in one or more small bowls on the buffet table. For each serving, put a lettuce leaf on one end of a softened rice paper and place a cucumber sliver and some mint and coriander leaves on top of the lettuce. Break the shrimp off one of the sugarcane sticks and place it on top of the vegetables. Begin rolling up the paper to enclose the filling. Fold in one end and continue rolling to form an open-ended cylinder. Dip the end of the roll into the dipping sauce and take a bite, then chew on the sugar cane for the sweetness (do not eat the sugar cane).

VARIATION If serving at the dinner table, set a small bowl of cold water and another of dipping sauce at each place at the table. Each diner makes his or her own rolls as follows (you might want to demonstrate): Set a rice paper on your plate. Dip your fingers into your water bowl and brush the entire rice paper generously with water. Let it sit until the paper is pliable and somewhat flimsy. Fill and wrap the rolls as above.

NOTE Sugar cane comes fresh and canned in better Asian markets; the fresh is scarce and very expensive when it shows up in the market, usually in early winter. If buying the canned version, check with the grocery clerk to make certain that you are buying the 6- to 7-inch-long stalks, not the cubes. If neither form of sugar cane is available, use a skewer or inexpensive bamboo chopsticks. Soak them in water overnight before wrapping them with shrimp paste.

CHICKEN WING ADOBO
(*Philippines*)

Adobo, the national dish of the Philippines, originally was a method of preserving. Generous amounts of vinegar, garlic, and pepper not only tenderize the meat but also add a pickled flavor and keep the dish from spoiling in the tropical heat. Chicken wings in an adobo sauce make great finger appetizers.

Serves 8

> 3 pounds chicken wings (about 18 wings)
> ¾ cup white vinegar
> 1½ cups water
> 3 tablespoons light soy sauce
> 6 cloves garlic, peeled
> 2 shallots, chopped
> 1 teaspoon coarsely ground black pepper
> ½ teaspoon salt
> 2 bay leaves
> 2 tablespoons vegetable oil
> 2 bunches fresh spinach, blanched

1.   Cut the wings into sections and discard the tips. Put the wings in a non-aluminum saucepan with the vinegar, water, soy sauce, garlic, shallots, black pepper, salt, and bay leaves. Let sit for 1 hour.

2.   Place the saucepan over medium-high heat and bring to a boil. Reduce the heat to low, cover, and simmer for 10 minutes. Remove the wings. Allow the cooking liquid to sit until the fat rises to the top; skim off and discard the fat. Bring the liquid back to a boil, then lower the heat to medium and reduce to ⅔ cup. Meanwhile, heat the oil in a skillet and brown the wings evenly. Return the wings to the saucepan to coat them with the vinegar sauce. Arrange them over a bed of blanched spinach. Serve hot or at room temperature.

PANAENG NEAU
Meatballs in Spicy Peanut Sauce (Thailand)

Panaeng Neau is the cocktail meatball of the '90s, standing in place of the once ubiquitous Swedish meatball. This recipe is another example of the versatility of the basic Thai red curry paste on page 18. Having the paste prepared ahead will make this recipe quick and easy.

Makes 24

> 1 pound ground round or other lean ground beef
> ½ cup flour
> ½ teaspoon salt
> 2 tablespoons vegetable oil
> 2 to 3 tablespoons Basic Red Curry Paste
>   (page 18) or prepared red curry paste
> 1 tablespoon paprika
> 1½ cups thick coconut milk
> 2 to 3 tablespoons chunky peanut butter
> 1 to 2 tablespoons palm sugar (see page 82)
>   or brown sugar
> 1½ tablespoons fish sauce (nam pla)
> 1 tablespoon coarsely chopped Thai basil
>   (horabha) or mint

1.   Shape the beef into 1-inch meatballs. Combine the flour and salt; roll the meatballs in the flour mixture and shake off the excess. Preheat a wok or skillet over medium-high heat; when hot, add the oil. Add the meatballs and brown them evenly, but leave them slightly underdone. Remove and set them aside.

2.   Discard all but 1 tablespoon of oil from the pan and stir in the curry paste and paprika. Fry lightly over low heat for a few minutes, stirring to prevent the spices from sticking and burning. Turn the heat to medium-high and add the coconut milk ½ cup at a time, stirring each time to thoroughly blend it with the paste. When all the coconut milk has been added, cook, stirring continuously, until red-stained oil rises to the surface, 5 to 10 minutes. Add the peanut butter, sugar, and fish sauce. Return the browned meatballs to the sauce and simmer for 5 minutes. Add the basil or mint and serve hot.

ROAST DUCK AND MELON SALAD
(China)

Salads combining meat, seafood, and poultry are becoming increasingly popular among modern Asian chefs. This refreshing summer salad is a perfect example, with the crisp yet smooth texture of melon and the sweet and sour flavors of other fruits offering contrast to the rich, meaty flavor of the duck.

Like *cha siu*, roast duck is traditionally purchased from a Chinese delicatessen ("roasting shop") rather than cooked at home. If you do not have a Chinese deli in your city, try ordering roast ducks in advance from a Chinese restaurant. In either case, tell them not to cut up the duck or you will get bite-size pieces, which is not appropriate for this dish. If you can't find Chinese crullers, deep-fry strips of won ton skin as a crisp garnish.

While the candied walnuts are essential to this salad, the Spicy Sesame Jellyfish Salad is definitely optional. If you are game for trying the jellyfish, remember to start by soaking it the night before.

Serves 8

½ *Cantonese roast duck*
1 *Chinese cruller or 1 cup fried won ton skin*
   strips
3 *green onions*
½ *cucumber*
4 *ounces jicama*
½ *honeydew melon*
½ *cantaloupe*
1 *mango*
1 *recipe Spicy Sesame Jellyfish Salad (page 119,*
   optional)
Juice of 1 lime
1 *tablespoon toasted black sesame seeds*

½ *cup Baked Candied Walnuts (page119)*
½ *cup fresh coriander leaves*

TOASTED SESAME DRESSING
2 *tablespoons Asian sesame paste*
2 *tablespoons warm water*
½ *teaspoon grated ginger*
2 *teaspoons sugar*
2 *tablespoons light soy sauce*
1 *tablespoon wine vinegar*
1 *teaspoon Asian sesame oil*

1.   Bone the duck and cut the meat with skin attached into shreds about ¼ inch wide by 1½ inches long. Blot any grease from the duck pieces with a paper towel. Set aside.

2.   Preheat the oven to 375°. Cut the cruller crosswise into ¼-inch slices. Place them on a baking sheet and bake until crisp, 3 to 5 minutes. Set aside.

3.   Cut the green onions into 2-inch lengths then cut them lengthwise into fine shreds. Peel the cucumber and jicama and cut them into 2-inch-long matchsticks. Peel and seed the honeydew, cantaloupe, and mango and cut them into ¼-inch by 1½-inch sticks. Chill.

4.   Prepare the dressing: Combine the sesame paste and water in a small bowl and mix until smooth. Add the remaining dressing ingredients and blend thoroughly. Taste for seasoning.

5.   If using the jellyfish salad, mound it in the middle of a wide platter with shallow sides. Put the duck shreds on top of the jellyfish (or in the middle of the platter if not using jellyfish). Arrange the green onion, cucumber, jicama, melons, and mango around the duck. Squeeze lime juice over the salad and pour the dressing over. Top with the sesame seeds, cruller slices, and candied walnuts, and garnish with fresh coriander. Toss together before serving.

BAKED CANDIED WALNUTS

2 cups walnut or pecan halves
3 cups boiling water
6 tablespoons sugar
¼ teaspoon salt
1 tablespoon peanut or corn oil

1. Cover the nuts with boiling water and let them stand for 3 minutes; meanwhile, combine the sugar and salt. Drain the nuts thoroughly and pat dry. While the nuts are still hot, combine them with the sugar mixture and toss to coat evenly. Add the oil and mix thoroughly. Spread in a single layer on a foil-lined baking sheet and let stand until dry to the touch, 20 minutes or longer.

2. Preheat the oven to 375°. Bake the nuts, stirring occasionally, until golden brown, 8 to 10 minutes. Serve warm or at room temperature. Stored in an airtight container, leftovers will keep for several weeks.

SPICY SESAME JELLYFISH SALAD
(China)

Jellyfish is best served as part of a Chinese "cold platter," the equivalent of the Italian antipasto course, along with such foods as sliced pig's trotters, cold poached chicken or pork, blanched vegetables, and wedges of "thousand-year-old" eggs. By itself, it doesn't have much flavor; however, the Chinese love its crunchy texture.

Serves 4 to 6

8 ounces dried jellyfish (preferably shredded)
½ teaspoon salt
1½ teaspoons sugar
1 tablespoon soy sauce
1 tablespoon white vinegar
2 teaspoons Asian sesame oil
Hot chili oil, to taste
Fresh coriander leaves, for garnish

1. Soak the jellyfish in lukewarm water for several hours or overnight. Rinse several times with fresh water. Drain. (If the jellyfish comes in sheets, cut it into fine strips at this point.) Return the jellyfish to the bowl and add boiling water to cover. Stir once and drain. Rinse well with cold water, drain, and chill.

2. Combine the salt, sugar, soy sauce, vinegar, sesame oil, and hot chili oil in a bowl. Squeeze the jellyfish dry and toss it with the dressing. Serve cold, garnished with coriander leaves.

FIVE-SPICE GRILLED QUAIL
(*Vietnam*)

Chinese five-spice powder—an aromatic spice blend of star anise, fennel, cassia, Sichuan peppercorns, and cloves—is often found in the pantry of a Vietnamese kitchen. These juicy, aromatically seasoned quail, with a nice sweet charred flavor from the sugar in the marinade, have become one of my favorite finger foods for buffets, or they can be served as a first course with the Chicken and Cabbage Salad on page 70.

Serves 6 to 12

> 6 quail
> 4 cloves garlic
> 3 green onions (white part only) or 2 shallots
> 1½ tablespoons sugar
> ½ teaspoon salt
> ¼ teaspoon black pepper
> ½ teaspoon five-spice powder
> 1½ tablespoons Vietnamese fish sauce
>   (nuoc mam)
> 1½ tablespoons light soy sauce
> 1½ tablespoons dry sherry
> Nuoc Cham Dipping Sauce (see Note, page 69)

1. Cut each quail in half lengthwise through the breast and along the backbone. With your palm press down on each half to flatten it.

2. Combine the garlic, onions, sugar, and salt in a food processor and chop finely. Combine with the remaining ingredients in a bowl. Rub the mixture all over the quail inside and out and marinate for 1 to 3 hours, turning occasionally.

3. Lift the quail from the marinade and scrape off the excess. Grill or broil about 4 inches from medium-hot coals or the broiler until lightly charred, about 7 minutes. Turn and cook until the juices from the thighs run clear, about another 7 minutes. Serve with rice and Nuoc Cham Dipping Sauce.

VARIATION Substitute 2½ to 3 pounds chicken wings for the quail and cook 4 to 5 minutes per side.

SAMBAL BHINDI
Lady Fingers Sambal
(Singapore)

I learned to appreciate okra in Singapore, where it is used in a variety of ethnic dishes. The Indians in Singapore refer to okra as "lady fingers" or *bhindi*; they stuff and stir-fry them and use them in curried vegetable dishes. This recipe is in the "Nonya" style—a marvelous style of cooking that emerged from the intermarriage of local Malay women with immigrant Chinese men. The okra is stir-fried with a typical *sambal* (a mixture of garlic, shallots, dried shrimp, and shrimp paste) spiced up with chiles and sweet-and-soured with tamarind. This is the recipe that converted me into an okra eater.

Serves 8

>   2 tablespoons dried shrimp
>   1-inch lump tamarind pulp
>   ⅓ cup boiling water
>   ¾ pound okra
>   2 shallots, minced
>   3 cloves garlic, minced
>   2 fresh red chiles, seeded and roughly chopped
>   3 tablespoons vegetable oil
>   1 teaspoon shrimp paste or anchovy paste
>   1 small head pickled garlic (optional),
>   coarsely chopped
>   1 to 3 tablespoons chicken stock or water,
>   if needed

1. In a small bowl, cover the dried shrimp with warm water for 5 minutes. Rinse well, drain, and coarsely chop; set aside.

2. Put the tamarind pulp in a small bowl and cover it with the boiling water. Mash the pulp with the back of a fork and let it stand for 10 minutes. Strain into a bowl through a sieve, pressing with the back of a spoon to extract as much liquid as possible. You should get about 3 tablespoons of tamarind liquid. Discard the pulp.

3. Trim off and discard the ends of the okra. Cut the okra into ⅓-inch-thick rounds. In a mortar, pound the shallots, garlic, and chiles coarsely. (You may use a mini-chopper if you prefer.) Set aside.

4. Preheat a wok or skillet over medium-high heat. Add the oil, and when hot, add the pounded shallot mixture, shrimp paste, dried shrimp, and pickled garlic; saute gently until fragrant but not browned. Increase the heat to high and add the okra; stir-fry for 1 minute. Stir in the tamarind liquid. If the vegetables are too dry, add a tablespoon or more of chicken stock. Continue stir-frying until the okra is tender but still crisp, about 8 minutes. Serve hot, warm, or at room temperature.

LOH BAAK GO
Pan-Fried Radish Cakes
(China)

Short of cooking it yourself at home, a good teahouse is the best place to try this wonderful, light, savory pan-fried pudding. A good radish cake should have a nice crusty outside and be moist and succulent inside, and it should still have the appetizing sharpness of the radish. All too often, they are gummy and pasty, but this version is not. Even non-radish eaters will find this appetizer very tasty.

Makes about 16 pieces

> *4 to 6 dried Chinese black mushrooms*
> *¼ cup dried shrimp*
> *3 Chinese sausages* (lop cheong) *or ½ cup*
>   *diced Chinese barbecued pork*
> *1½ cups rice flour*
> *1 teaspoon salt*
> *2 teaspoons sugar*
> *¼ teaspoon white pepper*
> *1 cup chicken stock*
> *1½ pounds Chinese radish, peeled and grated*
>   *(see Note)*
> *2 green onions, coarsely chopped*
> *Vegetable oil for pan-frying*
> *Light soy sauce*
> *Chinese mustard*

1. Place the mushrooms in one bowl and the dried shrimp in another. Cover both with water until soft and pliable, about 20 minutes. Squeeze out the excess water from the mushrooms. Cut off and discard the stems; coarsely chop the caps. Set aside. Drain and chop the shrimp; set aside. Steam the sausages (see page 13) for 10 minutes. Cool, cut into ¼-inch dice, and set aside. (Barbecued pork needs no steaming, just dicing.)

2. Mix the rice flour, salt, sugar, and white pepper together in a large mixing bowl. Add the chicken stock and mix to a smooth batter. Add the grated radish, mushrooms, shrimp, sausages, and green onions.

3. Lightly oil the sides and bottom of a 9-inch square or round cake pan. Pour the radish mixture into the pan; smooth the top. Tap the pan gently on the table to release any air bubbles.

4. Prepare a wok for steaming (see page 13). Steam the radish mixture over medium-high heat for 1 hour or until the tip of a knife inserted in the center comes out clean. Check the water level frequently; replenish often with hot water. Let the pudding cool, then turn it out onto a cutting board. Cut it into squares, rectangles, or triangles.

5. Preheat a skillet over medium-high heat and add a thin film of oil. When hot, add the radish cakes. Pan-fry until lightly crisp and brown, about 3 minutes on each side. Serve with soy sauce and Chinese mustard for dipping.

NOTE Chinese radish is a long, white, cylindrical root vegetable. It looks like a white carrot and tastes crisp and juicy, with the refreshing bite of a radish. The Japanese call it *daikon* and serve it grated with sashimi. The Chinese enjoy it in stews, where it becomes light and refreshing; it may also be steamed, braised, sauteed, boiled, or eaten raw.

KAI LOUK KOOEY
Son-in-Law Eggs
(Thailand)

I have yet to find a reasonable explanation of the name and origin of Son-in-Law Eggs. Both the name and the presentation—hard-cooked eggs, deep-fried and draped in a sweet, sour, and savory sauce—make this dish a conversation piece. They are traditionally made with chicken eggs, but quail eggs make perfect appetizer-size tidbits.

Makes 20

> *1-inch cube tamarind pulp*
> *⅓ cup boiling water*
> *4 tablespoons sugar or palm sugar*
> *3 tablespoons Thai fish sauce* (nam pla)
> *Vegetable oil for deep-frying*
> *20 quail eggs, hard-cooked and shelled*
> *2 red serrano chiles, seeded and cut into slivers*
> *3 tablespoons Crisp Fried Shallot Flakes (page 26)*
> *Fresh coriander leaves*

1.   Pour the boiling water over the tamarind pulp in a small bowl and soak for 5 minutes. Press the pulp with the back of a fork to break up any clumps and to help dissolve the tamarind. Pour through a fine mesh sieve into a small saucepan, pressing with the back of a spoon to extract all the dissolved pulp. Combine the sugar, tamarind liquid, and fish sauce in a small saucepan. Simmer until well blended and syrupy. Set aside.

2.   Preheat a wok or saucepan, add oil to a depth of 1½ inches, and heat to 360°. Fry the eggs in batches until golden and blistered, about 1 to 2 minutes. Remove, drain briefly, and arrange on a serving plate. Pour the sauce over the eggs and garnish with chiles, shallot flakes, and coriander leaves. Serve with toothpicks.

Son-in-Law Eggs

MISO BARBECUED
SHORT RIBS
(Japan)

This is not a traditional Japanese dish. But I like the way this cut of beef works with a Japanese-style marinade and sauce. Flanken ribs, beef short ribs cut across the bones into thin slices, are a very flavorful cut that works especially well in Asian-style barbecued dishes. You may have to order this cut in advance from your butcher.

For this and other Japanese-style marinades, I find the sweeter and milder flavor of a Japanese-style soy sauce such as Kikkoman more appropriate than other types.

Serves 6

> *2½ pounds beef flanken-style short ribs, ¼ inch thick, in sections with 3 crosscut rib bones*
> *1½ tablespoons Japanese white miso*
> *3 tablespoons mirin*
> *3 tablespoons Japanese-style soy sauce*
> *1 tablespoon white vinegar*
> *1 tablespoon sugar*
> *2 teaspoons Asian sesame oil*

GINGER TERIYAKI SAUCE
> *2 tablespoons saké*
> *3 tablespoons mirin*
> *3 tablespoons Japanese soy sauce*
> *2 tablespoons sugar*
> *2 teaspoons grated ginger*

1.   Trim and discard the excess fat from the ribs. Combine the miso, mirin, soy sauce, vinegar, sugar, and sesame oil in a large bowl; add the beef and massage the marinade into the meat. Marinate for 6 hours or up to overnight, refrigerated.

2.   Combine the sauce ingredients in a saucepan and bring to boil. Lower the heat and simmer into a light syrupy consistency. Keep warm. Remove the ribs from the marinade and wipe off the excess. Grill over hot coals or broil about 3 inches from the heat until seared, 1½ to 2 minutes per side. Serve hot over rice or noodles, with the teriyaki sauce spooned over the top.

SHRIMP AND POTATO TOASTS
(China)

Mashed potatoes give this traditional shrimp toast recipe a slightly heartier flavor. Shrimp toasts are customarily deep-fried; toasting them under the broiler is both more healthful and more convenient.

Makes about 24

> 1 French baguette or 12 slices stale bread
> ½ pound potatoes
> 12 ounces shrimp
> 2½ teaspoons salt
> 2 tablespoons minced Chinese chives or green
>   onions
> ½ teaspoon sugar
> ¼ teaspoon white pepper
> ¼ cup vegetable oil

1.   Slice the baguette diagonally into ½-inch-thick slices. Lay them on a tray to dry out. If using bread slices, cut 2 squares, triangles, rectangles, or circles from each slice.

2.   Peel the potatoes. Boil them until tender; cool and mash until smooth.

3.   Shell and devein the shrimp. Toss them with 2 teaspoons of the salt; let them stand for 10 minutes. Rinse well with cold water, pat dry, and finely mince with a cleaver or food processor. Put the shrimp in a bowl and add the potatoes, chives, remaining ½ teaspoon of salt, sugar, and pepper; mix into a smooth spread. With a butter knife, spread a ½-inch-thick layer of the shrimp mixture evenly over and to the edges of each bread slice. Brush the top with oil. Set the slices on a baking sheet.

4.   Preheat the broiler. Toast the slices under the broiler until lightly brown, about 5 minutes. Serve hot.

Shrimp and Potato Toasts

INDEX

Italic page numbers indicate photographs.